DELIVERANCE MEANS LOVE

Also by Audrey Harper:
Dance with the Devil

Deliverance Means Love

AUDREY HARPER

KINGSWAY PUBLICATIONS
EASTBOURNE

All the stories in this book are true.
Names have been changed to
preserve confidentiality.

Front cover design by Vic Mitchell

ISBN 0 86065 982 8

Printed in Great Britain for
KINGSWAY PUBLICATIONS LTD
Lottbridge Drove, Eastbourne, E Sussex BN23 6NT by
Clays Ltd, St. Ives plc
Typeset by J&L Composition Ltd, Filey, North Yorkshire

To John and Liz
who have taught me love.

Contents

	Foreword	9
1	A Night Call	13
2	Nowhere to Go	16
3	Idle Hands, Idle Minds	27
4	The Instant Age	35
5	Come into the Parlour	42
6	Deception Within	50
7	Gift or Counterfeit?	61
8	Let's Pretend	73
9	The Need to Fail	83
10	Warts and All	90
11	Best Foot Forward	99
12	Fact or Fantasy?	105
13	Like a Mighty Army?	112
14	Compassion: Storming the Gates of Hell	122

Foreword

There seems to be a feeling that somehow if you write a book it sets you apart from the rest of the Christians – you have made it. You have found the secret. As an author I know this is not true, and I know Audrey Harper doesn't have this attitude. She makes mistakes and is subject to human weaknesses like the rest of us, but she still seeks to help those in great need.

It is inevitable that not everyone reading this book will agree with every word. Some might react to specific areas, but please don't let this put you off. Think for a minute, 'Why am I reacting?' Consider whether you have something to learn. If in the end you disagree with some of the conclusions made along the way, please don't reject the core message of the book.

Sometimes Audrey has posed questions without reaching a detailed answer. Some of the questions may not have a well-defined and clear answer, but they will be summed up by learning what Jesus meant by 'laying down one's life' and that 'he came for the sinners'. The Holy Spirit came upon the church and made them witnesses – not just to the nice people but to the Samaritans, the outcasts that no self-respecting Jews would go near. Has it changed in our day and age? Surely the gospel is still for the outcasts and misfits.

Naturally everyone finds it easy to criticise and discover faults in others. Being involved with Reachout

Trust has meant I have received my fair share of criticism, and I know the same is true for Audrey. Some is valid, and we need to be humble enough to learn from it. But some is simply from people who have never 'been there'. There are glimpses here of Audrey's often sacrificial love and care for people who are not always receiving the necessary help from their local church. Audrey has 'been there' and so she can understand these people more than most.

Love and understanding are very powerful and we need to express them in our dealings with these people. James is one of the most practical writers in the New Testament, and it is no accident that we read 'be quick to hear, slow to speak' (Jas 1:19). The only way we will ever understand people is by first listening. Then and only then can we live the 'pure and undefiled religion' that James goes on to talk about. What is it? Reaching the poor and needy, the outcasts, the hurting, the misfits. When we meet their needs we are living true religion!

I want to make mention also of the attitude of certain areas of the press. Audrey, like others, has suffered at their hands. Some ridicule all 'proof' that is given concerning those who have suffered ritual abuse. They will probably say that the stories here that deal with this specific area are made up. One has to question whether much of what we read is really good journalism, because Audrey is one of those who knows beyond reasonable doubt that, in among the hoaxes and those needy people who invent stories of abuse, there are alarming numbers of genuine cases. As soon as a social worker feels that a life is in danger, he or she will act. But, as we have seen in recent cases, there may not be enough 'proof' to go to court and make a case. But the 'proof' is there, in these lives if not in court verdicts.

Not all the stories recorded in this book are about ritual abuse, but whatever the background and whatever the reason, the people are hurting desperately. They need others to accept them just as they are, and to love them continually until they are in a position once again to trust. Time and care are needed to give the Holy Spirit opportunity to work in a life, and the process is rarely helped by splashing the story sensationally across the front page.

Audrey also highlights the needs of those still at school. Many are experimenting with ouija boards, tarot cards, etc. On average, 30–50% of a class will own up to involvement with the occult. Berating them for what they have done will not help; we need to build bridges of love, not brick walls of condemnation.

In a day when most books are about living 'successful' Christian lives, we must ask the question: who will accept the failures? Who will help them when they fall again and again? Who will give them the atmosphere of love, trust and discipline they need?

This is what Audrey is seeking to do, and this is the message of her book. Reachout Trust is glad there are people like Audrey. But one man or woman – or even a few – cannot cope with it all. We need that mighty army. Please allow the Holy Spirit to speak to you through the pages of this book, and if you want to be involved in helping such people, do make contact with us.

Finally, if you see yourself in these pages and cry, 'I need help,' do contact one of the addresses found at the end.

Doug Harris
Reachout Trust
1992

Where other lords beside you
Hold their unhindered sway,
Where forces that defied you
Defy you still today;
With none to heed their crying
For life, and love, and light,
Unnumbered souls are dying,
And pass into the night.

F. Houghton.
© Overseas Missionary
Fellowship. Used by
permission.

1

A Night Call

The sound of the telephone ringing summoned me from my comfortable sleepy coma. Groping for the receiver and trying to wake myself up, I managed to say, 'Hello.'

'I can't carry on any longer,' came the voice of a near-hysterical young girl. 'I'm going to kill myself; it's the only way.'

Now I was wide awake. 'Hold on, let me use the other phone, then we can talk.' Leaving my husband John sleeping, I dashed downstairs. I glanced at the clock: twelve forty-five in the morning. It was going to be a long night.

'Can you tell me your name?'

Silence. Please, Lord, help me, I prayed silently as I tried to reach this young life that Satan was trying to steal.

'Never mind, you must know who I am, and I want to help you.'

A stifled sob and I realised that she was listening. 'Nothing can be so bad it's worth dying for—especially all alone.' Now the tears were flowing, and for a short while I could only wait. Again an urgent prayer: Father, please help me.

Now much calmer, my caller told me of her past life, a story I had heard many times before—satanism, ritual murder, blackmail, and the fear evident in her voice as she spoke.

'How come you rang me?' I asked.

'I read about you in a magazine,' she said. 'I've had your number for weeks but I was scared, and then tonight I found it screwed up in my pocket.'

'Have you taken anything?' I had to know; time might be short.

'No, I haven't!' And again she was sobbing. 'I don't really want to die, but I don't know how to live. Please help me.'

'God helped me to live,' I said gently, 'and his love is the same for you.'

Suddenly the voice rose hysterically. 'I've tried your way, and it doesn't work! They didn't believe me—I don't fit in. I'll never be like them . . . I'm so lonely.'

Her sobbing brought tears to my eyes, and soon I was crying with her.

'What are you crying for?' Her question caught me unawares.

'I'm crying for you, for your hurt and rejection.' A little laugh from my still unnamed friend. 'If you can't tell me your name I'll have to call you Polly.' More laughter, and then we were talking. The danger was over for now.

More relaxed, she listened as I shared with her the reality of a living Saviour—Jesus, the one who would never leave her. As she opened her heart to him I prayed with her. She was just nineteen years old. The road would be hard, but she would never be alone again.

'Will you trust me with your phone number?' A slight hesitation. 'Just so that I can ring you tomorrow and arrange help nearer to your home.' She gave me the information and added cheekily, 'My name isn't Polly— it's Susan.' We laughed together as I put the phone down.

It was two in the morning, but there would be no sleep for quite a while. The crisis was over, but I wept for Susan and for the church that had refused to hear her cry for help.

Now I sat quietly and I remembered. I thought of my years of darkness, serving Satan in fear. I recalled the time when in desperation I cried out to God, and of the seventeen-year struggle to know the freedom that only he could give.

I thought about my own battle, the constant running, the frustration, the yearning to be free and the reaction of the church, much of which I had recorded in the book *Dance with the Devil*. Neither Susan's story nor mine is unique. I get letters and calls from victims, some over fifty years old, who are still living in guilt and condemnation, and I begin to wonder if God has made a mistake in choosing me. Can it be that the church is still unable or unwilling to come to terms with satanism? Is ignorance preventing us from helping those who have lived and still live in darkness? Are our traditions more important to us than service? Do we really believe in a God who can change lives?

All these questions come pounding at me as I re-read a letter received that day. 'How can you call yourself a Christian after what you have been involved in? Signed, "A Christian lady".'

For a while I wallowed in self-pity. I thought of the two children whom I had brought into this world but could never be a mother to. I remembered the youngsters whom I introduced to a life of pain and darkness, and I wept again.

Knowing only one way to defeat Satan's taunts, I reached for my Bible. I read again the story of the cross, and those precious words in Romans 8: 'There is no condemnation for those who are in Christ Jesus.'

I looked at the scars on my arms, and I rejoiced. Jesus is real; God does not make mistakes; I am a new person. It is we, his body, the church, who must reach out to those still in darkness. We may get it wrong sometimes but, as I wrote back to that dear Christian lady, 'My God is bigger than all of us.'

2

Nowhere to Go

The promise of power

I was recently invited to a wedding, and it was great. Of course, I had a little weep; well, who doesn't? But for me there was a special reason. I had met Johnny in very different circumstances, and to see this handsome young man with purpose, pride and commitment, walking down the aisle with his new wife, was a treat.

At thirteen Johnny had run away from a violent home. He didn't know his real father, just a succession of male friends who kept his mother company. He had no idea where to go, so he headed for London. Alone and hungry, Johnny somehow managed to survive for several weeks on his wits, but he knew he couldn't dodge the police for ever: he needed somewhere to live and hide until he could change his identity.

Then his luck changed—or so he thought—when a smooth-talking man offered him a flat. He would have to share, and work to earn his keep, but Johnny wasn't afraid of hard work. He went to the flat, one of four in a large house, and although it was a bit tatty it suited him just fine. Johnny settled in quickly. His room-mate was a woman in her early twenties, friendly, but mostly out. He explored the house and got to know some of the other tenants, and he did any odd jobs that were needed. One couple he remembered well.

'They were a bit weird,' he recalled. 'But the thing I remember most was the smell inside their flat.' The couple often had visitors and during those times Johnny had to make himself scarce.

Johnny was just fourteen when his curiosity got the better of him, and he began asking his new friends what their secret was. They told him about their magical powers—how they could get whatever they wanted and were never short of anything. Of course, it was all very, very secret.

'I thought all my problems were solved,' said Johnny. 'I wanted that power whatever the cost. If only I had known.' His face pinched with pain as he remembered.

He was strung along for weeks, becoming more and more eager. Finally he was allowed to join—and his world was tipped upside down. He was sexually, emotionally and spiritually abused, and from then on was nothing more than a slave. He was trained for high priesthood, and he now admits that though repulsed by the sexual activities, some aspects thrilled him.

'I wanted to leave but I couldn't,' he said, reddening slightly. 'I hated myself, but I wanted the power. Besides, where else would I go?'

He began drinking heavily and, at nineteen years old, was sentenced to prison for violent behaviour.

I first met Johnny after his release, having been writing to him for several weeks. He had read an article about satanism in a Christian magazine and had written to the author, who passed him on to me.

Johnny longed to be a new man, but seemed unable to control his thoughts. He dwelt on evil, and admits that he was ready to become an abuser. He was still homeless and, with a prison sentence behind him, was finding it almost impossible to find work or digs.

'I kept thinking of the promises they made; if I carried on would I really be rich?'

I shared my own story with him, showing him how

false all the promises were, but I knew that nothing would change unless I could find him a home.

Finally, an elderly couple whose family had left home took him in, and on the day that I watched him walk down the aisle with Elaine, I knew that God had honoured that couple's sacrifice and had given them another addition to their family. Johnny had met Jesus. His mind was pure, his past forgiven. God had done a wonderful work.

Would Johnny have got involved in satanism if there had been somewhere to run to? I don't know. But I do know that satanists recruit runaways like him—the railway stations are full of them.

Flight from loneliness

I met Lisa on the streets as she was trying to cadge money from passers-by. I took her to a small cafe where we ordered breakfast. From the way she gobbled the food I knew it was some time since she had eaten.

Lisa had not run away, yet she was homeless. At sixteen she had just been released from a children's home, and she couldn't cope with the bed-sit that had been allocated to her. She had been in care for as long as she could remember, and was just not equipped to cope on her own.

When I left Barnado's I was not prepared either: I actually spent one month's pay in a day. Fortunately I was on full board at my job, otherwise I would have been in serious trouble. With a large chip on my shoulder I was not good company, and I could see in this young girl's defiance and anger the same attitude. To relieve the loneliness she spent most of her time and money in the West End of London, eventually losing her accommodation for not paying the rent. She was vulnerable to all sorts of vices, but because of my concern she agreed to meet me again. I was hoping that I could find her somewhere to live, preferably with a family who would show her what family life is all about.

A week later, as I stood waiting for Lisa in Soho, I remembered the years I spent on the same streets. The place looked cleaner, but I knew that by evening it would be full of society's misfits. The drug addicts would be waiting for midnight to collect their prescriptions from the all-night chemist; there would be call-girls, pimps, homeless—all going to make up a world that few of us ever see.

A tap on my arm brought me back to the present. As I looked at the pathetic girl in front of me I knew I had been right to be concerned. Instead of the bright if defiant youngster of a week ago, Lisa was cowed and dirty, with ugly bruises on her cheeks. The shock I felt was matched only by my relief that she had turned up. She seemed terrified, and begged me to get her away.

Where could I take her? I had already tried some hostels, but they operated on a first-come-first-served basis, and only after six at night. I couldn't imagine Lisa queuing up, and anyway, she needed somewhere to go during the day. I rang a doctor who had befriended me and he invited us to his home, where Lisa broke down and sobbed.

Ignoring my warnings she had started soliciting, and when invited into a car she went. She only began to panic when the unknown driver refused to stop. Worried and frightened she could only sit helpless as he continued driving—a cuff round the face silencing her protests. For the next twenty-four hours Lisa was held prisoner. My skin crawled as she talked about the people and things she had seen. I had witnessed the same ritual performed on a young girl abducted from the street for the purpose. I remembered the acrid smell, the noisy chanting, the physical pain. It was Hallowe'en. Satan had defiled another body, and destroyed another young life. It will be a long time before Lisa will be able to forget her experience.

So far from home

Andy was forty-two when I first met him. He was smart, clean and obviously wealthy. In fact I wondered why he had asked to see me, as he didn't appear to have any needs. Then he shared something of his life.

Andy had come from a good family; he had done well at school, and went on to college and then into the Army. He got married and became the father of three children. He was content.

All that changed when he left the service. He became restless and unable to adapt to civilian life. One job followed another and he began to drink heavily. Eventually his wife could stand no more and his children disowned him.

Andy drifted to London, with nowhere to go and no money. Night after night he would do the rounds of the hostels, hoping to get a bed but very often ending up in a shop doorway, or huddled round a fire with a group of meths drinkers, taking whatever was on offer—anything to deaden the pain. If you have no address you get no money, and without money there is nowhere to live. Life becomes a vicious circle, and in the end it is easier to lie down and die.

Andy finally sought help for his drink problem and was admitted to an alcoholic unit. After being dried out he was released—back on to the same streets. He was determined not to stay down, and began looking for a way out. Then he hit on the ideal job. He had seen the prostitutes and noticed how often they got beaten up; now he would offer them a deal. In short, he became a pimp, working not only with known call-girls but actually recruiting his own.

He deliberately searched among the homeless, and he hand-picked several girls, not even bothering to check their ages. Andy began to get rich on his takings, and was soon able to buy a flat. He got a job in a legitimate business and became a respectable member of society—keeping very quiet about his sideline. Then one of his girls was beaten up and gang-raped—she was fifteen years old. Until then they had just been girls, it was very impersonal, but as he looked at this broken, weeping lass he was reminded with a jolt that he had been homeless once, and here he was taking advantage of others in the same situation. He was devastated.

I guess many will see Andy as a greedy, evil man, but to me he was a victim. I can treat him with compassion because, but for the grace of God, I might have been abusing people myself, or still recruiting them from the streets to be abused by others.

Andy has a different job now, and he spends all his spare time on the streets seeking out those whose lives have been blighted. He takes them what physical comforts he can, and shows them in practical ways what a living relationship with God can do for those who are lost. Andy knows the joy of sins forgiven and, even as I write, he is gently reaching out to his family and praying that God will bring them together again to live for him.

Life in the gutter

Homelessness is on the increase, with family life breaking down, forced unemployment, the mentally ill being released into the community, youngsters leaving children's homes, angry and rebellious. Cardboard cities are springing up, not just in London, but in almost every major city. Hardened criminals, drug addicts, meths drinkers—society seems to be falling apart morally, emotionally and spiritually, and these are the victims.

Of course not every homeless person is going to get caught up in satanism, but they are all vulnerable. I was recruited because I was homeless. I was disposable, and no one would miss me and come looking for me.

At first I found living rough fun, but the novelty soon

wore off. I became flea-ridden and smelly—there's no running water on the street corner. I was often hungry, and in winter very cold, but if I thought that would melt the heart of the passers-by I was mistaken. Some walked by as if I didn't exist, others crossed the road, and occasionally someone would take the time to spit on me. Nothing they did could make me move on: I still sat in the gutter.

I looked forward to Sundays, not for spiritual reasons, but because it gave me the opportunity to get warmed up a bit. By visiting different churches as they opened I could guarantee at least three hours of warmth and, hopefully, sleep. Unfortunately some of the churches did not appreciate my presence. At one, the lady on the door insisted I must wear a hat, and actually produced a head-scarf. Can you imagine? There I am in dirty jeans and sweater, my hair matted with lice—and she was worried about a hat! I wrapped it round her neck, told her rather impolitely what she could do with it, and shuffled off.

Into another church, a bit gloomy, but nice long seats, ideal for a good kip. With no one on the door, entry was simple, and I chose a pew near the back. Everyone avoided me (probably the smell) and I fell asleep. I was woken by the polite cough of the man waiting to lock up, and I walked back on to the streets.

Not all the churches I visited behaved that way. There was one where free buns and coffee and a good helping of the gospel were always handed out.

I remember too, years later—in fact just a few weeks before my wedding—I was again homeless. I had been asked to leave a rehabilitation centre where I had been resident for three months. I was totally disruptive, and a bad influence, and their decision was probably right, but at least I had stayed long enough to get engaged to John. I had no money and no bed, but as John and I walked the streets we saw a church with lights on and went in. I told them my story and they agreed to pray for my protection. Then they wished us goodnight and showed us the door. John had to get back to the centre, and after he had left I felt a wave of loneliness. I was just contemplating which window to break in order to be arrested (which I sometimes did rather than freeze to death) when a gentleman from the church caught up with me. Pressing five pounds into my hand he said, 'It's all I have, but you might get bed and breakfast with it.'

Homes for the homeless

What can the church do? Isn't it a political problem? Surely it's the job of the welfare state to look after these unfortunate people? I am not a politician, but I am a member of the body of Christ, the church, and I believe that we have a God-given mandate to care for any-one who has a need, whether physical, emotional or spiritual—anyone who has fallen through the loopholes in the welfare state.

In Matthew 25:35–40 we read:

> For I was hungry, and you gave me something to eat, I was thirsty and you gave me something to drink, I was a stranger and you invited me in, I needed clothes and you clothed me, I was sick and you looked after me, I was in prison and you came to visit me . . . whatever you did for one of the least of these brothers of mine, you did it for me.

The task looks so enormous, and our efforts may seem like a drop in the ocean, but let's make a start. We can begin to support the many groups and individuals already working in this field. We can care, we can give and we can pray. Be careful though—I have found that if we are not careful, prayer becomes a cop-out, a reason for not actually doing anything. Get involved, then you'll pray.

Inner-city churches need to be encouraged. They are in the front line. If we can support them, they may feel able to open their doors during the day, thus providing a much-needed service. I know there would be problems—theft is fairly common—and I know that it takes a lot of commitment, willing volunteers and cash.

Those of us in rural communities may not have a homelessness problem on our doorstep, but why not twin with a city church? Many towns are twinned to somewhere abroad—why not the churches? (If you're in an Anglican church, there is already a scheme you can join, run by the Church Pastoral Aid Society.) We can then be involved in the front line, supplying the needs. Our church can learn a lot, our lives will be enriched, and the church we support can reach out to those in need. Sounds great, doesn't it?

I spent a week in Stoke-on-Trent a while ago, and was thrilled to see what one church was doing. A small four-bed annexe was being prepared as an emergency unit for the homeless.

'What's the good of four beds?' I can hear some of you asking. Four beds are better than none, and in fact when I rang my friend in Stoke recently he told me that the idea is catching on fast. The church now has a half-way house, two other churches have opened up premises, and a third is looking for a suitable building. The vision is growing. If every church in any town were to join the scheme, that's a lot of beds.

Schemes like these need co-operation—there must be no denominational arguments—but what a witness to the world! Satan would have no foothold as we serve in unity and love, meeting the needs of people where they are.

I don't always agree with handing money to the homeless, but how about taking them for a meal? This would bring the responsibility down to a very personal level. It would challenge our very faith. After all, it's one thing to send a donation—but what if you are confronted by a smelly, flea-ridden, half-starved human being? No, it's not easy to put your arms round them, or to be seen talking or eating with them. It's easier to

let someone else do it. God understands our human
weakness, but once we can admit our failings, and if we
are willing for the compassion of Christ to flow through
us, we will see such people as God sees them, and
serving them then is not difficult. When I suggest a meal,
I don't mean somewhere like Harrods or the Hilton—a
mug of tea and a doorstep sandwich will do nicely.

Long-term hospitality

And what about Lisa? Can anything be done for
youngsters like her? Thankfully most of the large
children's homes have closed down in favour of smaller
family units. But that doesn't take away the bitterness
and frustration that most of these youngsters feel. When
I left Barnado's I didn't know where home was. Having
never lived with a family I didn't even know how to
behave in a normal home. Maybe the time is right for
the church to offer long-term fostering. I don't know
exactly how we might organise it, but I do know that
there is a need for these youngsters to experience the
love and security of a family before they are too old to
appreciate it. How much nicer than a hostel or a bed-sit.
There is a desperate need for foster homes for older
children. Maybe you and I, after our own family have
left home, can think about taking on another child. It's
hard work, but very rewarding.

With mental hospitals closing down, many handicapped people are not coping. Imagine, after thirty or
forty years in one hospital, being put out into the
community—often quite a hostile one. It must be
devastating for them, and sadly some are ending up on
the streets. My own church plays host to one such group,
and they are lovely. How different was the reaction of
some wealthy citizens in a high-class area. They got up
a petition to make sure that a property in their district
was not used to house these unfortunate people. The

reason given? Their properties would lose their value. How can anyone value a house more than a human life? These people must surely be the least of God's children, and we are asked to serve them. Bewildered, confused, frightened, they can and do fall prey to perverts. If you have a group of mentally handicapped folk near you, visit them, take a cake with you, invite them out to tea— they love a treat. Make sure that they and their carers feel comfortable if they want to come to church. They may make a noise sometimes—ours do!—but it's great to have them. They have lots of love to give.

We are not going to solve the problems of homelessness overnight. Maybe what we do will seem very small and insignificant and we may never see the result of our efforts, but can we really sit and do nothing?

3

Idle Hands, Idle Minds

I stepped into the ground floor flat cautiously, my heart thumping so much I thought everyone in the building would hear it. The smell was almost overpowering and the rubbish lying around did nothing to raise my spirits.

'Hello,' I called, trying not to sound too frightened. 'Where are you?' The silence was deafening. I reached for a light switch and was comforted by the glow of a dingy bulb. I peeped into what turned out to be the kitchen, and then into the lounge. For a moment I thought the room was empty and then I saw them.

Seven or eight young people were slumped against the wall under the window. The blinds were still shut, but from the light in the hall I caught a glimpse of their faces, and I suddenly felt very cold. Their eyes were open, but they were not looking at me. It was as if a camera had captured a look of sheer terror on their faces.

My own fear was nothing compared with who or what had frightened this group. I sat quietly in one of the only two chairs in the room and prayed for wisdom.

The room looked like a bomb site, and I noticed that books had been torn or ripped apart. There were several markings in chalk on the floor, and half-burned candles stuck in makeshift holders.

This was not the opening of some horror movie; this

was a real place with real people. I had been called in by a social worker who had received complaints from others in the flats.

'Can someone put the kettle on?' I asked gently. 'I'd love a cuppa.' And with that I drew back the blinds. My quiet request seemed to jog them from their paralysis and they began to move.

'It was weird,' said one. 'Never known anything like it,' said another. 'Don't want to,' came another voice. Now they were thawing out and talking more freely. The story that unfolded began to sound familiar. A group of unemployed youngsters, to relieve the agony of having nothing to do and no money to do it with, had experimented with magic. Armed with books, mostly from the library, this group had spent weeks learning spells and incantations. When they thought they were ready they had met just before midnight to prepare, and as the time approached they took up their positions. Standing in a circle they began to chant.

'What happened?' I asked. They became agitated, and fear crept back into the voice of the one who appeared to be their spokesman.

'Nothing happened for quite a while,' he said, 'and then the room began to get very warm—it got so hot we could hardly breathe.

'We carried on chanting—we felt we were making contact, and we were desperate for something to happen. Then the door opened and there was someone there.' He flushed as he tried to explain.

'We couldn't see it, but we felt a presence. The door slammed shut and the room suddenly got very cold. Then a strange feeling went through us, and all of a sudden it was like everyone went crazy. We had to destroy everything, including each other.'

At this point the young man broke down in tears and the rest of the group seemed shell-shocked. Certainly they had destroyed virtually everything in the room, but each of them had also experienced a private taste of hell, and all of them needed help.

After I had arranged some help and counselling for them, we agreed to meet again when they were calmer. As I left I was both angry and sad: angry that such dangerous books are so readily available, angry that adverts, which promise everything, can be found openly on so many bookshelves, angry that occult magazines are so freely available in newsagents. How to get a job, how to make someone fall in love with you, a special charm to bring you luck, to make you rich. When you have nothing, it's so easy to be tempted. You read the advert, you try to get a copy of the book that it recommends— not difficult, the library will probably have it in the religious section.

And I was sad. Sad that intelligent young minds were being destroyed because there was no work for them, nothing to occupy them, no way of allowing them to be creative or challenged. I have visited several job clubs and talked to many unemployed people of all ages. Always there seems to be a feeling of despair. Lack of money, loss of dignity, and a feeling of uselessness are common. To fill the long days they may quarrel with their families, or turn for excitement and meaning somewhere else.

Work for idle hands

Gillian was highly intelligent and a good performer at school. She stayed on, planning a professional career and looking forward to university. But her grades were not quite good enough. Gillian was disappointed, but she rethought her plans and decided to study at evening classes and get herself a job during the day. Jobs were not easy to come by, and with so many leaving school it was first come, first served. Frustration turned to bitterness when she found she could not even afford her evening class. Gillian was on the dole. In her own words, 'I was just another number. They even took my identity away.'

Her mother recalls the gradual change in her daughter's attitude, and admits that Gillian became like a stranger in her own home. Haunted by the fear of never finding work, Gillian sought consolation with others in the same boat. She ended up using drugs and alcohol. 'People call us scroungers,' she said. 'Lazy idlers who don't want to work. But I *wanted* a job—anything to get back my self-respect.'

Then Gillian met some new friends. 'They were really nice,' she recalled. 'They shared everything they had and even offered me another home. The flat was fantastic, and I couldn't move in quickly enough. Now I could become someone.'

But there was a price to pay. Her 'friends' were from a satanic temple, and after a brief courtship they told her what her role was to be. Gillian wept uncontrollably as she told me, 'I wasn't even given a choice. It was join or die.'

It would be foolish to suggest that every unemployed person is going to join a satanic temple, but we need to be aware that satanists see the jobless as potential recruits and target them deliberately.

Young people need to feel valued, they need a challenge, and they want the opportunity to give to society instead of just taking. The occult is drawing them with false promises, subtle deception or outright abduction.

Misfortune-telling

I met Angie when she was waiting for a court appearance on a charge of shop-lifting. Her husband was already in prison, and the three children were due to be taken into care. Angie was witty, intelligent, and had obviously known better days.

Her husband Derek had been made redundant from a well-paid job, and at first they didn't worry too much. He had some redundancy money, and he would soon get another job—after all he had been with the same firm for over ten years and was a skilled worker. But at forty Derek was too old. Firms found it cheaper to take on youngsters. Fighting depression and trying to apply for jobs took up all his time, and Angie, desperate to help out, began to look for work herself. They sold their house, and after a short spell in temporary accommodation, which was a nightmare, they were allocated a council house. It was in a very run-down area, but they were in no position to pick and choose.

Gradually Derek was drawn into criminal activities, and was eventually sent to prison. Now Angie was on her own, and had to provide for the children. The welfare state was a wash-out. After she had filled in all the forms, they usually said 'no' to her requests.

Then Angie went to see a fortune-teller, who told her that she was going to come into a large sum of money. Poor Angie. Day after day she waited, and when nothing happened within a month, she returned to the fortune-teller. 'She told me again that I would be rich, so after that I thought I would order some things from a catalogue. When I couldn't pay I just sold the things and ordered more. Then when people gave me their orders I went and took the stuff from the shops.'

'You mean you believed the fortune-teller?' I asked.

'I don't know, but she offered me the one thing I didn't have—hope, and the chance to break out of the poverty trap.' The likelihood of prison weighed heavily on her mind, and the thought of her children in care made Angie shiver. 'And all because Derek lost his job.'

How can we judge the Dereks and Angies of this world? Who knows the pain and despair that they go through—the breaking point when crime seems the only way out?

Angie didn't end up in prison, and Derek is now at home with her. He still doesn't have a job, but is trying to retrain. It's not easy. I contacted a couple of churches in their area, hoping they could help, but Angie and Derek don't go to church and unless they do. . . . Maybe it's time we got out of the church, and met people where they are. If we sit and wait for them to come to us, we may have a long wait. Angie and Derek were shocked at the thought of asking the church for help. But why should they be? We are the hands and feet of Jesus—would he have left Angie and Derek alone?

A welcoming church

I was at a series of meetings, and was thrilled on the first night when several people said they wanted to give their lives to Christ. Among them was Mark, a young man, scruffy in appearance and a bit smelly. When he left he assured me he would be back, and next day there he was, sitting on the step waiting for the church to open. I thought at first that it was my preaching that had caused him to be so keen, but when I asked him he said, 'I have nowhere else to go. When I became a Christian I couldn't carry on the way I was. You see, I was living with and working for a homosexual, and God showed me that it was wrong, so I walked out. I've been sleeping rough and now I have no home and no job.'

No wonder he sat on the church step. The church responded wonderfully, and soon Mark had a new home and a job. He wasn't made to feel embarrassed; people just quietly went up and offered what help they could.

What is the attitude of your church? Do you honestly make unemployed people feel welcome? Do they feel like equals in the church? Do you have a social fund, a small account that will enable you to give them a treat occasionally? Could you pool resources and send someone for a week's holiday? Could those who have

caravans lend them out? Could someone good at cooking
make extra cakes? Could you push the odd ten pound
note quietly through a letter-box? Look around and see
who needs to be blessed.

The joy and pleasure that we can give unemployed
people cannot be measured, but I know from personal
experience how it feels.

When my husband John lost his job I watched him
change overnight. From a humorous, dedicated husband
and father he became paranoid, tense and angry. He
refused to answer the door, and was ashamed to be seen
outside during working hours in case people thought he
was a scrounger. His whole nature changed, and the pain
I felt for him was unbearable.

Then one morning we heard a rattle on our letter-box.
I found an envelope addressed to the family with one
hundred pounds inside and a short note telling us to go
on holiday. Nothing was signed, and I never found out
who it was, but I can assure you the effect was
marvellous. We enjoyed our holiday, but the best thing
was the feeling that we were not alone—somebody cared
about us. However small your contribution may be, it
can bless people, and helps to pick them up when all
seems lost. By our attitudes we can help others to find
security and salvation in Jesus, or drive them to seek an
answer elsewhere.

Make sure that you don't behave as one church I came
across. A group of unemployed people regularly sat at
the back of the church and were never asked to do
anything. They were not invited to any outings, nor were
they asked to help with the Sunday school. When I asked
'What's wrong with them?' I didn't expect the answer I
got, and for a while I was left speechless.

'We feel that if they are not working, they shouldn't
be involved with the children—they might influence them
adversely. And as for outings, well, we felt that they
couldn't afford it, and we didn't want to embarrass them.'

As I probed further it came out that one of this group was a trained youth worker whom most churches would have been thrilled to have in their congregation. What a waste!

Not all churches are big enough to help with the government-funded work training schemes, but we can all offer something on a smaller scale. How about asking an unemployed person to keep the church premises clean, or do gardening for some of the congregation? You don't necessarily need to pay cash—pay them in kind, with groceries or electricity stamps or an evening out. We need to treat the unemployed with dignity, so that at least within the church family they feel they have something to give.

> Suppose a brother or sister is without clothes and daily food. If one of you says to him, 'Go, I wish you well; keep warm and well fed' but does nothing about his physical needs, what good is it? In the same way faith, if it is not accompanied by action, is dead (James 2:15–16).

4

The Instant Age

In with the crowd

'Audrey, will you help me?'

The request came from an anxious teacher friend of mine.

'If I can,' I responded. 'What's the problem?'

'One of my fifth-year girls has arrived at school with what I am sure is a satanic Bible, and wants to know if I can explain what it is. She has been very difficult for the last six months—not at all like her usual self.'

I was at the school to do a talk on drug addiction, which the fifth year were studying, so armed with my notes and my own experience I faced thirty-five curious fifth formers.

I recognised Jane immediately—sullen, angry and obviously trying to be disruptive. As I shared my own pain about drug abuse and mentioned briefly my encounter with satanism, Jane became quiet and thoughtful: she was listening.

I answered questions and, when asked, shared my experience of the living Jesus. Jane asked no questions at all until the others had left.

'Show me your arms,' she demanded.

I knew why and quickly rolled up my sleeve. My arms are not a pretty sight—scarred by self-mutilation and collapsed veins from shooting heroin—but in that

35

moment they seemed beautiful: Jane had the proof she needed. For a moment she stared in horror, and then a tear trickled down her cheek. 'Can I talk to you? I'm in such a mess, and I don't know what to do.'

Jane's problems had started seven months before. 'Life was so boring. I enjoy my school work, but apart from that, what is there to do? My parents don't like my dress, my friends, my music. They call me a rebel and . . . well . . . I just decided I might as well be one.'

Friends introduced Jane to drugs, which she didn't enjoy very much but it kept her in with the crowd.

'But two months ago things got really weird. There was a lady we knew who suggested we all wear black clothes and sit in a circle. I didn't want to, but she gave me a pill and then I didn't care. She began doing really scarey things like talking to someone who wasn't there. I wanted to stop going, but I couldn't—I just kept turning up. I hated myself, and that made me angry. Then one weekend we met for a party. The lady in black produced a book and told us to take an oath on it. I couldn't. I just grabbed the book and ran. That's why I brought it to school—I wanted to know what it was.' Jane was shaking now, and fighting back the tears. She had begun to realise how close she had been to something horrific.

I shared with her again the reality of Jesus; how he gave his life for her and for me, so that we might know life to the full. I linked her to a church, knowing that though she must find Jesus for herself, she would nevertheless need other people to help her. As for the black book, I had the privilege of burning that.

Bored to death

'I'm bored!' Two little words which I hear so often. Children during the long summer holidays; teenagers when the batteries on their ghetto blasters fade; housewives with husbands at work, children at school and so many labour-saving gadgets; even senior citizens dreading retirement and wondering how they will fill the long hours. Boredom must be the major sickness of our society. And boredom can drive us to create excitement for ourselves.

I recall the story of a happy and intelligent fifteen-year-old lad who had won a place at a top boarding school.

During one term his parents received a phone call to say that he had attempted suicide. Desperately worried, they took him home where he rested for three months before going back to school. After a few weeks he tried to take his life again, and this time was admitted to a psychiatric unit. That was when his parents found out about the ouija board club. His schooling was virtually over, his career prospects all but ruined. Today he is still moody and depressed, and the damage done will take years to put right. And why? Because he and some friends got bored.

An altered state . . . or a mess?

Joan is a young housewife and mother. Her youngest child started school and suddenly she had time on her hands. 'I just didn't know how to fill the day,' she said. 'I got bored.'

When a friend suggested a new experience Joan was ready. 'It was just a bit of fun,' she recalled. 'We went to a demonstration on personal awareness, and it was good. I stayed behind to talk and they told me I was gifted, and encouraged me to join a group of like-minded people to enable me to reach my full potential. I really enjoyed it at first. Meditation and relaxation left me feeling good. I was taught how to ease myself into a subconscious state and then I was encouraged to find my other self. It was odd—like being on a different level—

but of course I was in control and could alter the state
whenever I liked.'

Gradually Joan began to despise her old self, and
longed to be free to live on her new level. Very often
she would find herself slipping from one to the other,
much to the dismay of her family. Gradually she began
to resent the family for their demands on her—they were
stopping her from attaining her higher self. She could
only see one way out of her dilemma. 'If I die then I
can't be accused of neglecting my family. And I can live
my new life for ever.'

The medium and the message

I was taking a service in Somerset once, and two elderly
ladies who were part of a spiritualist group who used the
same hall found themselves at my meeting by mistake.
They were distressed when I shared about my time
in the coven and the powers I had been given, and
the Holy Spirit began to show them that something was
wrong.

Both ladies were bereaved, one just recently, and
the other had taken her friend to a medium to try to
contact her loved one. Now, after hearing what God
was saying, she was worried. Who were the mediums
contacting?

We discussed it together and concluded that it
certainly wasn't of God. And since there are only two
sources of spiritual power, it must be Satan. I was
curious as to how these two ladies had gone to the
spiritualist group in the first place.

'I was bored,' said one of them. 'When you live on
your own there isn't much to do, and they were singing
hymns so I thought it was all right.' Two dear friends,
helping each other, but both walking the wrong way.
That night God made himself known to them, and they
left the hall rejoicing.

'I want it, and I want it now'

Boredom can also be the means of leading astray those who are in the church. We had a friend who was for ever looking round for something new. Every crusade, every new speaker, there she was in the front row. Finally she announced that she and her family were going to set up their own church, as all the other churches had nothing to teach her. Now she is heavily involved with New Age teaching, and the tragedy is that she can't tell the difference.

Our friend wanted instant change in her church. How many of us today fall into the trap of wanting things to happen instantly? Television means instant entertainment; videos come in all shapes and sizes so that at the flick of a button we can be amused; we have instant food, instant romance by computer, portable phones for instant communication. Everything, it seems, can be achieved at the push of a button. Is it any wonder that people become bored when life is reduced to pushing buttons? We do not know how to think for ourselves any more, and we are afraid of silence.

I remember as a child learning to read so that I could amuse myself. I remember playing in a meadow of freshly-cut grass, building dens, or making play houses. What fun I had with discarded boxes! They became buses or dolls' prams—whatever I wanted. Today's toys are designed to give instant gratification, with no creativity or patience needed.

Some time ago we decided as a family that we would try to do without the television for a while. For the first two days we were almost in mourning as we sat looking at the empty space, hardly speaking to each other. But gradually we began to look for other ways to spend an evening, and we talked, read, played games together— all the things that we used to do when our daughter was young. We found we had rebuilt our family relationships.

I am not against television, but I think a night off occasionally does us the world of good.

It is so easy for us in the church to develop this desire for instant gratification. I know that I am not a saint and that I get things wrong. When I cried to God I know he heard and answered, but the change in me was not instant. The miracle of God's love is instant, but the working out in our lives certainly isn't.

I am always concerned when I meet those people who have no church fellowship, but spend their time going from one event to another. They must see miracles every week or they haven't been blessed. They must see the wrong things in the church put right instantly, or they leave and move on elsewhere.

Instant answers

Bess was heavily involved in New Age philosophy—she was totally self-sufficient and had no need to ask help from anyone. Then she became seriously ill with cancer, and suddenly all her abilities seemed useless. At twenty-six she was afraid of dying. She couldn't depend on her own faith—it was letting her down. I visited her often because I loved her dearly despite her strange beliefs. I shared my faith with her. I told her of a living God who would accept her just as she was, and slowly Bess began to reach out to Jesus. The effect of this was beautiful. Bess became calm, and radiated peace to all who visited her. I introduced her to a local church, thinking that she would benefit from the fellowship. I wish I hadn't bothered.

I got an urgent request from the hospital to visit her and, thinking the worst, I left my family and rushed down to see her. Gone was her peace and her will to live and she was refusing treatment. What had happened?

It seemed that the church fellowship I had introduced her to was very progressive. They believed that if they

asked God for something he would answer immediately.
When they prayed for Bess and she was no better they
concluded that it was her lack of faith. She must refuse
further treatment and show that her faith was real.
Confused and angry Bess challenged me. 'I thought you
said that God accepts me as I am.'

'I did and he does.'

'Well why won't these people accept me as I am? They
don't like me being ill—I'm an embarrassment to them.'

I didn't know how to answer her. Those people wanted
instant results.

I stayed with Bess and shared from the Scriptures with
her. I talked to her of the spiritual healing that God had
given her. Bess died, but not without hope, and not
without peace.

Let's not be deceived in the church into looking for
instant answers and instant success. God has a purpose
bigger than we can ever imagine and it may take a
lifetime to work it out.

5

Come into the Parlour

A bit of fun

Maria was fifteen years old when she went with some friends to Blackpool.

'Of course, we all had our palms read, and the lady told me that I wouldn't live beyond thirty-five. I laughed at her. I didn't believe it, and anyway, thirty-five was ages away—pension age.'

Maria forgot about the prediction and carried on with her life, but every year, when her birthday came round, she found herself remembering what the palmist had said. She didn't want to—it just happened. At thirty-four and a half she was so frightened of how she might die that she wanted to end it all herself. She had refused to marry in case something awful happened to her. A young girl had some fun, and now was reduced to contemplating suicide.

I met Maria when she came to a meeting I was conducting, and she admitted that we were her last hope. If we couldn't help her she would carry out her plan to kill herself.

After introducing her to Jesus, the only one who could help her, I prayed in his name for her freedom. The relief was immediate, and that night the chains that had bound her for so long fell away. Maria is now happily married with a young family, and has discovered that Jesus can meet her every need.

Maria was not a devil worshipper; she hadn't set out to look for Satan, she just didn't recognise his games when she saw them. Our image of Satan is the one portrayed by Hollywood: a monster, half human, half animal, with a long tail, two horns and wielding a three-pronged fork. His followers have black cloaks, pointed hats, black cats, warts on the end of their noses and a broomstick to fly on at night. The picture is one we first encounter in kindergarten, and Satan is quite happy for us to go on believing it.

The truth is that satanists do not walk around looking grotesque—they look like you and me.

The occult is about the seduction of minds and the controlling of thoughts, leading to emotional, physical and spiritual bondage and eventually to eternal death. People don't have to believe in Satan to play his games, but the damage is nevertheless devastating.

I have met so many young people who have started out having 'a bit of fun' with a ouija board, tarot cards, fortune-telling or some other seemingly innocuous pastime, only to discover that the door has slammed behind them, and there is no way out of the nightmare.

'It's only a game'

I had just finished a lively, noisy lunchtime debate in a secondary school. As the bell went for resumption of classes I gathered my papers together and thought of the well-earned cup of tea that was awaiting me.

'Hey, Miss, Brian's crying.' An urgent tug at my sleeve brought me down to earth. Brian, aged fifteen, was looking pale and frightened, and some of his friends didn't look too good either.

'The bell has gone,' I said gently. 'You'll be late for lessons.'

'I can't go,' whispered Brian. 'I feel ill. One of us is going to die and I don't know who.' By now he and the two girls with him were shaking. I sat them down and asked someone to fetch a teacher.

The story that followed was sad, but not unique. A group of five youngsters had met regularly at Brian's house after school. No parents were around, and they had decided to play with a ouija board.

'We've been playing for several months,' he explained. 'We talk to Jim—he's a friendly spirit. In fact he's almost one of us. He likes us. But two weeks ago he said he was lonely and needed a companion. He said that one of us would die at a party, but he wouldn't say which one. It was as if he was laughing at us, but we didn't dare stop playing in case he got mad.'

By now a teacher had arrived. 'But why do you play with ouija boards?' she asked.

'It's only a game,' was the unanimous response. 'Only this time it's gone wrong.'

Things went wrong for Harry, too. I was called when he was discovered running round a school playing field, screaming uncontrollably. When I stopped him he was deeply shocked and very frightened. Perspiration ran down his face and he was shivering violently. As he calmed down he told me what had happened.

A group of fifth-formers had made a ouija board and decided to try it. None of them believed it had powers— it was only a game.

'The marker began to spell my name,' said Harry. 'I thought it was one of the others doing it, but no one was touching the board. I couldn't move, I was so scared. The board was talking to me. Then the marker spelled out the name of my best friend, followed by the words: kill him. I just flipped.' Harry was embarrassed now, but he and the rest of the group insisted I took the board away.

The ouija board is not a game. It is the first step into occult activity, and the results can be disastrous.

And now, your homework . . .

Micky was just fourteen and was already running a tarot ring in his school. I found out when other pupils came for help; they were scared stiff. I wanted to meet Micky and left several messages, but he was afraid. Then one Sunday night he turned up outside church wanting to talk.

'How did it start?' I asked gently.

'A teacher told us to investigate fortune-telling for our homework,' he replied. 'I didn't know where to start, so I got a magazine on horoscopes from the local newsagent. There were all sorts of things advertised—rune stones, crystals, tarot cards—and I didn't know which to order, so I sent for the lot.' Micky admitted that he had stolen the money from his parents, £50 in all, and lied about his age on the form he had to fill in.

Once he had taught himself the basics Micky took his ideas to school. There were plenty of willing volunteers among his mates to join him.

'I didn't really *believe* it all, I just thought it was fun.'

But Micky became hooked.

'I have two spirits in my bedroom,' he said quietly. 'One is friendly, but the other one frightens me and tells me to do awful things.'

'Such as?' I prompted. He gave me a long look—and then shuddered.

'It tells me to kill my parents.'

Micky was in a bad way—high on drugs, pale, drawn and anxious—but he wouldn't let me help him.

'Ring when you're ready,' I urged, and gave him a contact number. Micky never rang. Today he is an adult involved in fully-fledged satanic rituals. I continue to pray.

I have heard other incidents of homework being set on the occult. In fact one teacher admitted that if he set work on this subject, he could guarantee that the homework would get done.

'There is great interest and curiosity in this subject, and if it gets the work done, so what?'

My own daughter, at the age of twelve, was asked to produce an essay which invented a religion, with a god, rituals, prayers, and so on—but not using anything from the Christian faith. I'm afraid I didn't have the courage to go to the school and complain; I simply kept Liz at home so that she didn't have to hand the homework in. When I eventually plucked up courage to go to see the teacher I was appalled by her response. 'Children must learn to do as they are told.'

'Fine, then you won't mind me telling yours to play in the middle of the motorway.' I was angry. This was the deputy head—what about all the children who would pass through her hands?

Fortunately not all teachers think like this, and many are realising the need to be careful, but if we are parents we need to be prepared to get things changed if necessary.

It's in the stars

The occult always seems so innocent. Horoscopes are everywhere, in newspapers, magazines, children's comics—we even get it with our breakfast on early morning television. Public figures, film stars, heads of state, all use astrology. For some it is a bit of light reading, but others base their whole lives on it, and the astrologers become rich on their gullibility.

People who read horoscopes and live by them are opening themselves up to forces over which they have no control. What is behind it? Satan. And he's not stupid: he'll get it right often enough to keep people playing his game.

'I only read them for fun,' said a dear lady of seventy. 'I mean, they don't really work, do they?' Flossie had been housebound for many years. What a price she paid for her bit of fun. The horoscope told her not to go out, it could be dangerous. Of course Flossie went out and met with a minor accident. From that time she became a prisoner to 'the stars' and blamed herself for not heeding the warning. Unless the column actually said 'go out', Flossie remained indoors. Eventually she developed agoraphobia.

Dear Flossie is just beginning to live again. Slowly she is regaining confidence and, thanks to a caring church, she is finding that Jesus really does love and care about her. It will be some time before she can enjoy life to the full.

And then there was Mary. After her husband died Mary wanted to sell her house and move to somewhere smaller. She was understandably feeling vulnerable, and when she saw an advertisement for an astrology reading she went, believing it would help her make the right choices. Mary was told that under no circumstances should she sell her house for three years; it could prove harmful to her. Thankful that she had sought advice, she took her house off the market and waited. It was a very unhappy time: memories brought on bouts of loneliness and the financial worries were very real. Three years later Mary discovered that she would now have to sell well below the original price because of a slump in the market, and if she didn't sell immediately she would probably never get a buyer.

Mary went back and challenged the astrologer. His reply? 'Well, you don't know what might have happened to you personally if you had sold earlier.' This veiled threat was enough to frighten Mary badly, and she ended up receiving psychiatric help.

Death means freedom

'Audrey, listen to this.' Simon was trying to persuade me to listen to some heavy metal music.

'Come off it, Simon, you know I don't like it.'

'But I want you to listen to the *words*,' he said, with a look of concern.

As I put the earphones to my ears the noise hit me, and I screwed my face up in agony. After what seemed like ten minutes, but was in fact two seconds, I ripped the earphones off and admitted defeat. If I was to get hold of the words, I would have to try some other way.

I admit that I don't enjoy some kinds of music, but I don't condemn them. Music is a personal choice, and I don't suppose today's music is any more peculiar than that of the fifties and sixties. What does concern me is how some groups promote themselves and their music. Outrageous behaviour is nothing new—scandal sells, both music and books—but when groups resort to promoting devil worship we need to beware.

Through a friend I was able to obtain a heavy metal music magazine, and the words of one song in particular appalled me:

> Candles glowing, altars burn:
> Virgin's death is needed there.
> Sacrifice to Lucifer,
> My master.
> Bring the chalice,
> Raise the knife,
> Welcome to my sacrifice.
> Plunge the dagger in
> Her breast;
> I insist
> SACRIFICE.
> Demons rejoice:
> Sacrifice,
> Sacrifice.

(Lyrics from a song by Slayer.)

This is a description of a real ritual in a satanic temple. It doesn't matter whether the group are devil worshippers or not—they are still promoting satanism, and it's sick. Would you feel comfortable with your child singing this song? The fact that the words can't be understood the first time round doesn't matter. Most young people admit that the more they play songs, the more they pick up the words. So many young people spend all their free time with walkmans plugged in.

And what about music that promotes death? Can it really affect our minds?

> Life, it seems, will fade away,
> Drifting further every day.
> Getting lost within myself,
> Nothing matters, no one else.
> I have lost the will to live,
> Simply nothing more to give.
> There is nothing more for me –
> Need the end to set me free.
>
> *(Lyrics from a song by Metallica.)*

See the occult promise: death means freedom. It's a lie! Newspaper reports reveal that at least two young people have committed suicide as a result of listening to this song, and ten more have signed a suicide pact. We don't find life by looking at death—we find life by accepting Jesus, the author and giver of life.

As Jesus said, 'The thief comes only to steal and kill and destroy; I have come that they may have life, and have it to the full' (John 10:10).

So many have been drawn into something which seemed harmless, but which proved to lead into bondage and fear. When people live in fear, that is not of God.

Satan wants to prevent us from finding and worshipping the true and living God, and he will use every means in his power to draw us into his kingdom of darkness and fear. Let's be aware of the many ways in which it is possible to walk all unsuspecting into his traps.

6

Deception Within

'Hey, Miss, can you give us a demonstration?' The question came from a young lad trying to look big in front of his class-mates. I looked round this group of thirty fifth-formers. A lively debate had been going on for nearly an hour and still they were firing questions at me. I knew that many of them were searching for truth, and my heart went out to them as I remembered my own painful search. I prayed silently that none of these would walk the path that I had travelled as Satan's partner.

All too soon the lesson ended and I was left looking through some advertisements that the pupils had collected.

'Send for the magic Buddah,' said one. 'Rub its back and you will have all the money you want.' 'Learn the magic spell and whoever you fancy will fall in love with you.' 'Magic to get rid of an unwanted partner.' I began to appreciate how the youngsters felt: it was all a bit confusing.

I chuckled as I thought of some of the points they had raised as we tried to discover how real these promises might actually be. Few of us are exempt from greed and at the thought of all that money the mind boggles. During the debate we had concluded that the promises were false. As one lad pointed out, 'There wouldn't be enough money to satisfy us all, would there, Miss?' The fact that the item in question cost ten pounds also aroused suspicion, but despite this, and even though we agreed that it was a con, several admitted that they would try it if they got desperate.

We laughed at the idea of using magic to get a date, trying to work out the possibilities if we all fancied the same one, but again several of the class, girls more than boys, said that they would be tempted to try. These young people already have some knowledge of and sympathy with the occult.

Society today is breeding dissatisfaction and insecurity, and many are searching for a meaning to life. I spent one evening just watching advertisements on the television, and I began to understand some of the pressures that are put on us every day. You know the sort of thing: a certain aftershave and all the girls will follow you down the street; the right deodorant, girls, and you will never be without a boyfriend. And if your favourite chocolates have not been delivered by a superman who crosses ravines and swims oceans, they are not worth having. By advertising standards I was a failure. My coffee was not up to scratch, I'm using the wrong brand of butter, and *my* hair looks like wire wool! Was I doing *anything* right?

And it's not just television. According to the glossy magazines I'm too fat, too short and have too many pimples; my diet is out of this world, and I wonder how I survive at all. How many youngsters will spend their life trying to become a perfect specimen?

Can you see the subtle way in which our minds are being conditioned? Keeping up with the neighbours becomes, without our realising it, normal behaviour. Is it any wonder that we are never truly satisfied and have to keep on searching?

I was shocked at the reaction of my young school friends when I suggested that Jesus had given me the answer to life—that he himself is the only answer.

'What's he got to do with it?' said an angry voice. 'Who is he anyway?'

To them, religion is OK for others, but not relevant to them. Few of them went to church, and it was written off as dead, dull and boring. Some even felt that the church was no different from the occult: it asks for money, wants to change them, and it makes promises that it can't keep. I have found this reaction many times as I have visited different schools. Is it time to ask why?

Error in the church

Why is the church not reaching people with the simple truth of the gospel of Jesus Christ? When I was searching for God, feeling empty and desolate and confused, I used to think that the different messages I heard were due to denominational differences. Is that so? Or is it that we are preaching more than one gospel? Are we altering the truth slightly in order to make it sound more attractive? We may not do it deliberately, but we need to be aware of the temptation. Most cults have started with verses from Scripture and have then built their 'gospel' round them. The Moonies, Christian Scientists, Jehovah's Witnesses—all are taking people out of the truth and into bondage by their use of the Scripture. Of course we may all see things slightly differently, but in the end if we don't preach truth we will never see the captives set free (John 8:32).

Jesus says, 'If you hold to my teaching, you are really my disciples.' How much we need to become submerged in the Bible and to take hold of the spiritual feast that it offers in order to recognise and overcome Satan's deliberate but very subtle infiltration into the church.

Multi-faith services

How many of us have attended a multi-faith service? In the name of spiritual unity it's all the rage at the moment, but how can we allow those who worship false gods to stand in our churches with us and pray with us?

I appreciate the need for tolerance, but Jesus himself said, 'I am the way and the truth and the life. No-one comes to the Father except through me' (John 14:6). Jesus does not, and never will have, any other names, and in our multi-faith society we need to be uncompromising in our attitude and in our practice.

The New Age in the church hall

The teaching of 'the New Age' sounds great: let's look after the planet, conserve nature, and have love and peace with all. It teaches that God is within us; in fact we can become God if we find our higher self. Many companies are advocating meditation techniques for their staff, and others have prospective employees' hand-writing analysed. But what is more worrying is that some churches are allowing the use of their buildings for yoga, meditation and the teaching of Eastern arts. Check who is hiring *your* hall: a few pounds' income is not worth the broken lives that will follow.

Alternative medicine

I cannot say that all alternative medicine is evil, but I would say that just because something makes us feel better does not make it right. Just because royalty, famous stars or Members of Parliament condone some-thing does not make it right. Many people believe that all natural medicine has been collected by witches, cursed and then handed on to us. While white witches do use herbs and natural ingredients, and some may put a curse on them, many large companies now collect or produce their own, and compared to today's modern drugs I would rather use the natural remedies—and sometimes do. Before trying alternative medicine, check out the spiritual source. It may, for example, stem from Egyptian or Eastern mysticism. Go back to the Bible and be sure you know what you are getting into. If you fear you have been deceived then confess it to God and ask for his help; he withholds nothing from those who seek him.

Freemasonry

Over the years the church has given freemasonry a respectable face. For some of us that was not deliberate: we didn't know what it promoted or where its roots were. I don't pretend to know everything now, but I do suggest that you read a book on the subject, preferably one written by an ex-mason (like *The Craft and the Cross* by Ian Gordon, published by Kingsway). Some of the initiation rituals remind me forcibly of things I have experienced in satanic temples. Let's not condemn people, but do let's help them to face up to what they believe and where their loyalties lie.

Health and wealth

Imagine you are crippled with arthritis, absolutely broke, and very depressed. A minister in your church preaches about health and prosperity: 'By his stripes you have been healed. Therefore if you are sick it's because you are allowing Satan to attack you. God is bountiful and longs to give.' So if I'm hard up it means that I am not living in the centre of God's will? Let's examine this teaching carefully.

John and I heard a message like that once and we were devastated. John had lost his job through ill health, and I was crippled following a fall. We left the church in despair, but once home, we began to search the Scriptures—partly to prove the preacher wrong, I admit, but also determined to find the truth. The more we read, the more we realised that it is possible to preach half truths. I found examples of those whom God chose not to heal immediately, and others who were most definitely poor. I read about Job: he lost everything, was covered in boils, and yet God knew all about it and allowed it to happen. Even though he restored Job to great prosperity, he allowed a time of suffering and poverty.

In John chapter five we read about the man at the pool of Bethesda. Jesus singled out one man; he could have healed the whole lot, but he didn't. I don't know why, but one day I will be able to ask him. Paul had a 'thorn in the flesh' which may have been a physical ailment, and after pleading three times for God to remove it, he accepted that he would have to live with it. If we are not healed instantly, could it be that God has another purpose?

Before you begin to think that I'm doubting God's healing power, I want you to know that after suffering two strokes in quick succession, I too have received miraculous healing. I'm not denying healing—it's just that God has his own purpose and time for each one of us; all he asks is that, like Job, we remain faithful.

My friend had a stroke and was left crippled, but her ability to love and serve God astonished her neighbours, and people would seek her out just to be with her. I popped in for a visit one day and found her very depressed. She had been listening to a Christian tape.

'What am I doing wrong?' she cried. 'God hasn't healed me. Why?'

I was watching a television programme on healing, and a young girl admitted that she felt so guilty when she wasn't any better after prayer that she resorted to lying about the pain. I know just how she felt; I've done the same thing. It was easier than having to face those who assume that you must be sinning, or have no faith. If we have to lie to one another, how can we be honest with those who are searching?

Physical healing is a wonderful thing, but how much more precious are emotional and spiritual healing, and how much more urgent is the need to know that our eventual home is with God in heaven. It is essential to know that my sins are forgiven and that one day I will meet God face to face. It is not essential that my body is in perfect condition when I die—I'll be getting a new one anyway! Let us be careful not to bring others into condemnation because they are ill. Don't get angry if God does not seem to hear your prayers and answer them instantly. Whatever our condition God's love never changes—and nor should ours. We live in a fallen world, and the germs that fly about land on whom they will— they can't tell the difference between Christian and non-believer. If you feel poorly wrap up and go to bed, but don't feel guilty. That only pleases Satan, not God.

Get rich quick

I joined a satanic coven because I was promised everything I wanted. Young people admit they would try magic to get rich. Can you see the danger of preaching that God promises prosperity? Can we anyway preach prosperity to a nation where unemployment is rising, businesses failing and more and more people are falling into the poverty trap? Let's do as Jesus did and feed the poor—not tell them they shouldn't be poor.

Paul best sums it up for me in Philippians chapter 4: 'I am not saying this because I am in need, for I have learned to be content whatever the circumstances. I know what it is to be in need, and I know what it is to have plenty. I have learned the secret of being content in any and every situation, whether well fed or hungry, whether living in plenty or want.'

My daughter, Liz, at the age of eleven was taking her prayer life very seriously. After she had spent nearly all day on her knees—not the usual thing—curiosity got the better of me. I stood outside her door listening (I don't normally recommend this!) and was just in time to hear her thank God for her new pony. Since a pony was not on my shopping list, I thought I ought to check this one out.

'The minister said that God will give us our heart's desire,' she said almost defiantly when I asked her. 'And I want a pony more than anything else.'

A childish misunderstanding?

Sheila was certainly no child. I had known and admired her as a Christian for two years. After hearing the 'prosperity gospel' for the first time she stopped coming to church. When I next met her she seemed upset.

'It's all a big con,' she said. 'God hasn't given me my three-piece suite, and I've been waiting for it to be delivered.'

I must have looked blank because she hurried to explain. 'My old one was falling apart, and after what the minister said I went home and threw it away. The trouble is that now I don't have anything to sit on.'

The sad thing is that through that misunderstanding, and the fact that she didn't get what she wanted, Sheila turned her back on God. The effect on her family has been devastating. She is now divorced and a very bitter lady.

God is not a puppet, where we can pull the string to get supplies. He is a loving heavenly Father who cares for us and knows what is good. Often he supplies through his people—you and me. God wants us to be generous, not grasping. Our teaching affects our attitude towards others. If we struggle to keep up with a false, materialistic view of prosperity, we become competitive within the church, which is very sad.

I was speaking at a church in Wales, and after the service an elderly lady kept me for some time. Daisy had never been involved with occult things: her only crime was that she came from a very poor part of town and no one ever went to visit her. She felt trapped by her poverty, and was deeply ashamed of her appearance when in church. I wept for and with Daisy, but the answer lay with her church. As soon as they realised the problem they acted, and now Daisy is the most spoilt lady in town.

Should people like Daisy have to ask? Or should we

be more sensitive to others? It would be lovely if, whatever their state, people felt so secure in the love and fellowship of God's people that they could discuss their needs, whether physical, financial or spiritual.

Positive thinking—positive mess

One day, while out shopping, I bumped into an old friend. She was in agony and I could see why. A large, angry boil on her neck prevented her from holding her head upright. Trying to be helpful I suggested that she see a doctor and get it lanced.

'"What we confess with our mouths . . .",' Jane grimaced. 'I haven't got it, and I won't accept it.'

I was amazed and said bluntly, 'Well, that's tough, because *I* can see it and *you* can feel it, so it *must* be there!' I left her quickly in case I got a lecture on being 'negative'.

Positive thinking, or 'mind over matter' as it is known in occult circles, would be funny if the consequences were not so serious. A dear friend threw her drugs away after being told to be positive, and died in a diabetic coma. We have all been given common sense, and if God has done a healing work we can take time to have things checked by a doctor. God is not going to undo his work.

I have met several people who believe in positive thinking, not just in health but in every aspect of their lives. But we still get sick, we still have to go to work, and I have found that this teaching makes me covet things that are not mine.

I was complaining to a friend about my lack of space: 'I only have a two-bedroom bungalow—the council won't give me three bedrooms. It's plenty for our needs, but I would love an office.'

'That's soon rectified,' she said. 'Look around, and when you see what you would like name it, claim it in Jesus' name and you'll get it.' I thought she was joking.

'Do you really believe that?' I asked, my mind doing overtime. I was mentally making a list and greedily adding to it by the second. Then with a shock I realised that this was another of Satan's lies. We can't go round claiming other people's property. This teaching encourages greed, and I have never found any scriptural basis for it. It is on our knees that we claim things from God. The battle is a spiritual one, and there are no short cuts.

The whole truth

In Luke 24:47 we read that 'repentance and forgiveness of sins will be preached in his name to all nations, beginning at Jerusalem'. We don't always mention the need to repent. I have listened to many appeals and I thrill to see people responding to the gospel. 'Come to Jesus and he will meet your every need.' I agree. But I well remember responding to an appeal like that and it caused heartache for me and the minister. I was in pain and desperate. I asked the man to pray for me, and he said that I needed to put things right with God first. I hit the roof and stalked off. The poor man wondered what was happening. If he had mentioned repentance in his appeal I probably wouldn't have gone forward. He hadn't lied, but by leaving out one word, I felt that he had cheated me.

Repentance is more than being sorry. It is a deep regret for things done or not done, and a turning round and walking a new path, acknowledging that we can't do it on our own. It is a complete surrendering of our lives to God.

In *Dance with the Devil* I don't mention repentance. At the time I cried out to God I didn't understand much—all I wanted was to stay alive. I couldn't appreciate what Jesus had done, what it had cost him, and Satan was determined to keep it that way. I didn't have a clue about relationships. With no family background I had to learn as I went along. My relationship with God was stormy: I got angry when I was caught, yelled at him when things went wrong, and in between I ignored him.

Repentance became real for me at my deliverance. As the evil chains that held me snapped, I looked at the empty cross; I wept at the knowledge of Jesus' great sacrifice for me. He chose to die even though I allied myself with his greatest enemy. Jesus willingly lay down his life so that I might live. Truly I repented.

Satan is crafty, and with so many searching for truth he is giving them many choices. Let's examine our own hearts before God, and examine too what we are preaching as truth in our churches. Let's repent of all that is not of God and ask him to help us start pushing back the dark forces that are taking over our land.

In 2 Timothy 4:3 we read: 'For the time will come when men will not put up with sound doctrine. Instead, to suit their own desires, they will gather around them a great number of teachers to say what their itching ears want to hear. They will turn their ears away from the truth and turn aside to myths.' The gospel of Jesus is complete and can set captives free. But if we don't preach the truth, where will people hear it?

7

Gift or Counterfeit?

'Audrey, can you advise me?' The question came from an old minister friend of mine. 'I've been trying to help a young girl, but lately she's moved to another church and I'm concerned about her behaviour.'

Knowing that Don was not given to jealousy, and would only want the best for the girl, I agreed to meet him.

Denise had been involved in ritual abuse since the age of two, via her step-father. It continued even though she was taken into care at the age of twelve. She maintained that she had been aborted three times, and was accusing social workers of being involved. At seventeen she was admitted to a psychiatric unit and stayed there for two years.

Don's difficulty lay in trying to check the story without causing Denise any more pain. I agreed to meet her as soon as possible, but first I needed to know why Don was so concerned.

It seemed that while attending his church, Denise was making good progress. Then a couple turned up who insisted that they had a 'deliverance ministry'. The church didn't see much of Denise after that. She was in trouble with the police for stealing, and when Don tried to talk to her, she said that she couldn't help herself—it was an evil spirit. Don gave me the name of the new minister, and I agreed to speak to him and hopefully to meet Denise in person.

As things worked out, I met Denise first. She invited me to her bed-sit, and as I looked around I was amazed at the quality of her belongings. For someone unemployed it was pretty expensive stuff.

Denise seemed to be in a dream world, not knowing the difference between fact and fantasy. The story she related did not tie up with what I had heard from Don, and she couldn't—or wouldn't—look me in the eye.

I decided to find out what I could about Denise's new church and on checking with friends I found I had reason to be alarmed. It was a free church, not affiliated to any denomination, and had been set up by a couple who had tried every other church. I always worry about spiritual gypsies; they are not usually happy about submitting to authority, and can tend to make up their own rules. It would appear that the social services had been called in at one point by worried parents whose children talked regularly about casting out demons—they even practised on each other—and had become quite violent.

I felt I needed to speak with the minister of this church quickly. I rang him and told him who I was and of my concern for Denise.

'Oh, you don't have to worry about her, she's serving in the church. In fact she has an amazing ministry—it's almost as though she can see right through people.' I could well imagine what gift she was exercising. I had been right to be concerned.

I tried to talk about Denise's problems. 'Yes, we know about her past. It's amazing—we've cast out a thousand demons, and there aren't any left.'

'I didn't know there were so many about,' I remarked, trying to cover up the real fear I was feeling.

'Yes, my wife has been used greatly in this ministry. She has even spoken to Denise's dead babies—in the spirit, of course—and they told us that Denise has three still alive.'

I was asked politely not to interfere, but I was angry.

No wonder the poor girl was confused and back in hospital again.

Several months passed, and then I had a call from Don suggesting that we go and visit Denise together. After her release from hospital she had gone back to his church.

As soon as we walked through her door, Denise began rolling round on the floor, heaving and screaming.

'For goodness' sake, girl, I've only come for a cup of tea. Go and put the kettle on.'

Embarrassed, she did as she was asked. Denise was so used to falling down, or 'manifesting', that it had become a habit. She imagined that Christians expected it of her.

The damage done to Denise was severe. She couldn't face reality; every problem was 'an evil spirit'; she had no concept of free will or self-discipline and she lived only to please herself.

When I challenged her about the stealing she admitted to it. She liked pretty things and couldn't afford them on her dole money. Under her bed were boxes of catalogue goods which she had no hope of paying for. We agreed with her that they should be returned. At least now she was using her free will. What she needed was a job, wise counsel and a stable church.

That couple who ministered to Denise could see nothing wrong with what they were doing. They were not malicious—they loved Denise—but along the way they had allowed themselves to be sidetracked by the supposedly more 'glamorous' elements of deliverance.

In 1 John 4 we read, 'Dear friends, do not believe every spirit, but test the spirits to see whether they are from God, because many false prophets have gone out into the world.'

Notice that false prophets have already gone out, and as we are being urged to test the spirits, we can assume that some of these have found their way into the church.

I suppose that we in the church can be divided between those who don't believe demons exist at all, those who see them everywhere, and—probably the vast majority—those who through fear or ignorance ignore the subject at all costs.

In Revelation 12 it says:

> And there was war in heaven. Michael and his angels fought against the dragon, and the dragon and his angels fought back. But he was not strong enough, and they lost their place in heaven. The great dragon was hurled down—that ancient serpent called the devil, or Satan, who leads the whole world astray. He was hurled to the earth and his angels with him.

Satan and his angels are the enemies of God. They seek to destroy all that is good, and if that means deceiving not just the world, but the church as well, they will do it.

True or false?

When we think of counterfeit gifts we think of mediumship, clairvoyance, words of knowledge, precognition, automatic handwriting, and so on, and we declare that we do not have anything to do with them. But if we misuse the spiritual gifts that God has given the church we open the way for Satan to use these too, and what should be good and upbuilding becomes harmful. And because Satan is subtle, we don't realise the damage that we are doing.

I have had ministers call me and ask how they can prevent satanists from attending their churches or conferences. We can't. So we need to recognise them for what they are—not an easy task.

Satanists are not impressed by gifts they can counterfeit. They prophecy, heal, and most speak in tongues, albeit satanic. But when the supernatural power of God is demonstrated, they tremble. Can we distinguish between the two? Can we recognise false tongues and gifts that are operated in the flesh?

The gift of tongues

The first time I heard tongues in a church I fled, thinking that my old dancing partner had caught up with me. The voice was chilling and hard, becoming more and more hysterical, and was followed by a deathly silence.

I believe that we often confuse the gift of tongues with praying in tongues: they are different.

Paul tells us in 1 Corinthians 14:22 that the gift of tongues is for a sign; not to those who believe, but to unbelievers. I heard a story once that illustrates how God uses this gift.

At a meeting in a well-known church in London a tongue was given which, without the giver realising, was pure Arabic. Some Arabs in the meeting recognised their language and, even before the interpretation was given, fell on their knees before God.

I have had the privilege of attending a church where the gifts were operating in love and power, and I know that they can set hearts on fire. Different people gave messages in tongues, but each time the interpreter was on his feet immediately—no hesitation, just strong, direct and powerful words; there was no mistaking God's voice. If we don't have the interpretation, the tongue is of no use or, what is worse, we take a guess at the interpretation and the message is wishy-washy and vague.

Paul also reminds us that if the whole church should speak in tongues and an unbeliever walks in he will assume that we are all mad. Prayer and worship used together bring a special anointing, and when all the voices rise together in tongues a precious time of fellowship is often enjoyed. But wisdom is needed in an open meeting. I have seen people leaving meetings before the word is preached because they are fearful of

the sound of speaking in tongues. They may never
return.

Satanists will from time to time visit a church to size
up the opposition. One girl I spoke to admitted that she
had given a message in her own (satanic) tongue, and
after a short time someone 'interpreted'. It was nothing
to do with the given message, but the church went away
happy. She agreed that if she had been challenged she
would have left the meeting—but no one challenged her,
not even those in authority.

Not every Christian has the gift of tongues, and many
don't speak or pray in another language. I believe that
if we are not careful we can put too much emphasis on
the spiritual gifts and not enough on the fruit of the
Spirit. Many more people come to Christ through seeing
the fruit than from experiencing the gifts, and it is worth
remembering that while Satan can imitate spiritual gifts,
he cannot produce spiritual fruit. If we go back to a more
biblical dependence on the Holy Spirit we may not be
duped quite so often.

Deliverance

I was urged by a friend of mine to attend a meeting with
her, and I have never been so ashamed or embarrassed
in my life. Some four hundred Christians gathered
together for what I thought was going to be a sound
Bible study. Instead we had a lesson in how to cast out
demons. The demons came in all shapes and sizes, and
with every name under the sun: spirits of nicotine, sex,
even bad breath! Anyone who had anything wrong with
them had a demon cast out. They screamed, shouted,
laughed—I had never heard anything like it before. Even
in a satanic temple the noise and confusion were not so
bad. I never want to see that again.

Whatever happened to overcoming the flesh, growing
in grace, maturing in Christ? I tell you that public
displays of this sort do not glorify God. They give Satan

all the attention he seeks. Several months later I met a lady from that church, and she was in a pitiful state. She turned up on my doorstep, carrying all her belongings in a plastic bag. As I let her in she took one look at John and began screaming. Now, John may not be the best-looking guy around, but he's not that bad. I realised that Kath was very poorly and needed to be in hospital; she had suffered a complete mental breakdown. All she could talk about was demons; they were, she informed me, coming out of the soles of her feet. Apparently she had failed a missionary course at the church and the subsequent guilt had devastated her.

I know of one girl who didn't remember what had happened during her deliverance; she was just thrilled to be free in Jesus. Imagine her horror when a 'helpful' church member told her what she had done. She is now too embarrassed to go to church, and although she is free, she has no fellowship and could very easily fall away.

Deliverance is not just about shouting to demons while pushing the poor victim to the floor. Demons are not deaf. Shouting may build up our courage, but we can end up causing mass hysteria. We must not treat this sort of ministry as a peep show—it is not entertainment.

Nowhere in Scripture have I found that Jesus used strong-arm tactics against the enemy. He used simple words of command and the demons did as they were told. He acted with the authority given him by his Father, and he has passed that authority on to his disciples. In the story of the demonised man in Mark 5 we can see how Jesus dealt with casting out demons. In this example Jesus is dealing with more than one spirit, but when he hears there are many he does not stand there for hours calling them all out individually. He banishes them and they leave and enter a herd of pigs. The life of that man was changed. People who knew him and had been afraid of him saw him sitting at Jesus' feet. He didn't have to make an appointment for more ministry, and Jesus didn't have to probe and prod to get answers. Nor do we read that Jesus touched him.

We have all the authority that Jesus had, but unless our lives are right before God we cannot use it. Casting out demons was for Jesus a normal part of his ministry, and so it should be with us. We in the church need to grow up, learn to overcome the flesh, and not blame Satan for everything.

While deliverance should come quickly, we need to remember that emotional healing normally takes months or even years. So counselling may be a long-term affair—concerned not with casting out demons, but with encouraging the person to grow in grace and walk in the Spirit.

The Christians in that church I went to wouldn't have recognised a demonised person if they had seen one, and Satan isn't going to announce himself. There are so many people living in darkness, whose only hope is God, and if we his children spend all our time casting demons from each other, we will never hear their cries for help.

Possession—or oppression?

The question arises, can a demon live inside a true Christian? Notice I say 'inside'. I know that Christians can be affected by demons on the outside by oppression, but distinguishing between that and possession is very important—it affects how we pray. Oppression and depression are very often confused with possession, and yet all three are different. I have not found anywhere in the gospels or epistles instances of a Christian or a church member being possessed. I have heard it said that Peter was possessed because he tried to stop Jesus going to the cross, but Jesus said 'Get thee behind me, Satan,' not 'Get out of Peter, Satan.' Peter was trying to prevent what had to happen because he loved Jesus, and in that moment Satan moved in and Peter's love became Jesus' temptation.

In Mark 16:9 we read that Mary Magdalene was the one 'out of whom he had driven seven demons', but we need to note that this is the past tense. Jesus had delivered her from the demons so that she could become his follower.

Notice in Scripture that the demons always recognise Jesus first—we need more of him and less of self.

Satan and his army use our minds and our flesh to sow their seeds, and the sin inside us is only too willing to assist the growth. If we as believers have not yet learned to resist the devil, sinful acts will follow as we give in to the flesh. Sin is within us, demons only stimulate it from the outside.

If we could mature properly, much of the so-called deliverance ministry wouldn't be needed. If we as Christians believe that we are living under Satan's power, if we run here, there and everywhere for deliverance, we are never going to be able to help others. If we walk close to God and feed on his word we won't fall prey to the enemy quite so often.

The night I was set free I knew it. The job was done. I didn't have to keep going back for more ministry. What I had to do was close the back door, and look to Jesus for the power and authority to overcome. It didn't happen overnight. There were days when the oppression was awful, and I still faced torment. And of course my emotions took a long time to heal, but God had started work and with the help of my minister I learned to study God's word, and lean on his promises. Deliverance means a changed life, changed attitudes and a new heart. With God's help I shall go on changing.

Words of knowledge

How often have you had someone bring you a message and you are doubtful about it, but because of the words

'God says,' you dare not consider it might be wrong. If I had accepted every word that people have had for me, I would have been sent all over the place, running around and achieving nothing. Satan would love that.

I find it best to check through Scripture and ask God to confirm his word—he doesn't mind—and usually within a week someone or some circumstance will confirm the word or otherwise. I try to be gracious and not destroy the confidence of anyone who has been mistaken. We don't want to deter people from beginning to use the spiritual gifts, but neither can we afford to take on a counterfeit word. We need to remember that it is possible to use the gifts in the flesh.

I listened one day as two ladies had an argument. Words of 'knowledge' flew backwards and forwards, all about forgiveness and pride, and I began to think these two were the only ones God was speaking to. Then another lady stood up and said in a clear voice, 'I don't know who this is for, but God says "Do it."' Imagine if I had been planning to rob a bank! Or, tragically, if someone had been contemplating suicide. The result could have been disastrous. It's always best to wait on God a while before jumping up with a word. If it is from him a few minutes won't matter, and if it's not, then let it go.

And have you ever challenged a word of knowledge? I have. In one meeting where I was speaking, a man kept standing and shouting out Scriptures. At first I thought how spiritual he was, then I began to see that though the words rolled off his tongue, he didn't seem to know what they meant. With the authority of Christ I asked him to be silent, and he stopped. After the meeting he told me that he had never read a Bible in his life. He wasn't into the occult—Satan was just using an empty vessel.

Prophecy

The New Age equivalent of prophecy would be medium-ship or clairvoyance, automatic handwriting, precognition, divination, telepathy. It is important that we know how to test things by the word of God.

If a message seems selfish, then beware. Selfishness is occult, not Christian—our message is one of service. And what about the meetings where so many messages are flying around that there is no time for the sermon? Be careful, if Satan can prevent us from being fed, he will, and however spiritual the meeting seems to be, the gifts do not come before the word.

'Slain in the Spirit'

This is all the rage just now, and I have dealt with people who have been in tears because they have not fallen down; they felt that they had missed a blessing. The Bible tells of men falling down in the presence of Almighty God. It speaks too of awe in the presence of his glory and his holiness, and of lives transformed for ever.

But what we see today is people getting up after a few minutes exactly the same as when they went down. (I actually witnessed one young man who, while on the floor, politely moved to let someone else fall, and then got back down himself!) We do need to make sure that we are not expecting everyone to do it to order. Our spiritual walk, while involving our emotions, also calls us to faith.

Let the truth set them free

Our nation is being flooded with occult lies and many people are believing them. It's time the church told the truth about God and the result of rejecting him. Maybe we need to tell people about hell. If they don't know where the lies lead to, they have no reason to turn away from them. God is merciful, I know that. But he is also just, and one day we will stand before him for judgement.

This is not a popular gospel, but it is the truth. Can you remember when you last heard a sermon about sin? There's no need to preach hellfire every week, but we must not take our salvation for granted, and if ever there was a time to teach these things it is now.

Satanists believe that the devil is co-equal with God, wrongfully banished from heaven and waiting to be restored. It's a lie—they haven't read the end of Revelation. But who is going to tell them? They must hear the truth before they can decide.

New Agers believe that they can become God, pagans worship many gods, and they all believe in reincarnation. They are on their way to hell. It is a real place—I've stood on the brink, smelt and seen the evil. Let's reject Satan's lies, test the spirits, preach the word of God and see captives set free.

8

Let's Pretend

When we first acquired a telephone I learned something
new about human nature. Whenever I answered the
phone I changed my accent and went all posh. It came
to a head one day when even my own daughter didn't
know who I was, and I realised that if people wanted to
speak to me, then I should sound like me!

Why did I try to sound like someone else? Did I think
that changing my voice would make me more accep-
table? People always listen to posh voices, don't they?
What rubbish! As if an accent is going to change me.

Since I became a Christian, God has changed my life,
my heart, my attitudes; but I'm still Audrey Harper,
common and happy. In my travels I see many in the
church family struggling to be something they are not. If
only we could relax and be ourselves our Christian lives
would be much easier, but the need to be accepted, and
the fear of rejection if we don't conform, force us to act
a part.

When we become Christians we are like babies, and
we have to begin at the beginning. Many of us had hardly
ever been to church before we met Jesus—we don't
know how to behave. So we copy the others. We sit
when they sit, stand when they stand, pray, sing—it's
quite an adventure to begin with. But copying can have
its dangers. We might try to copy the most spiritual
person, or the one with the most obvious talents. But

how do we judge who is spiritual, and what standards do we set?

The first time I listened to Billy Graham preach I longed to be like him and serve God as he does. And if I had a voice like Cliff Richard there would be no stopping me. We all have our dreams, and most of them stem from the need to be accepted. You and I are not famous, but we are important to God and he is the one who matters. It is our very uniqueness that makes us special, so how sad that so many of us spend our Christian lives trying to be someone else.

Ephesians 5:1 tells us who to copy: 'Be imitators of God, therefore, as dearly loved children, and live a life of love, just as Christ loved us and gave himself up for us as a fragrant offering and sacrifice to God.'

The one place where we should feel comfortable is in our church fellowship. We don't need to act a part there, we can be our real selves. We don't have to fight for acceptance there. Or do we?

The occult is drawing people who, for one reason or another, dislike themselves or their circumstances. They get on the treadmill of false promises, but all the magic in the world is not able to change them. Fear of rejection makes them constantly try to hide their true selves, and fear of being found out brings them into awful bondage. We *must* show the world that whatever people are like we will love and accept them as Jesus has accepted us.

Maureen the missionary

Way back when I was at school I had a friend called Maureen. She was a devout Christian and didn't mind who knew it. She longed to be a missionary—and she practised on us. She would pick her target and move in for the kill. One week she selected me. She moved her desk to sit by me, and every break there she was, Bible in hand, waiting to preach. Now I was pretty naughty at school, and every teacher had a report on me, but Maureen was convinced that I could change, and even told the teachers so, much to my embarrassment. Finally I decided that the only way to get rid of her was to play along, so next Scripture lesson, for which we had to learn a Scripture passage off by heart, I was word perfect—much to everyone's surprise. (I can still remember 1 John 1, and even today if I want to impress someone I quote it!)

For a whole week I did nothing wrong, and Maureen decided that her fervent prayers were beginning to work. But instead of now leaving me alone she redoubled her efforts. She invited me to a Youth for Christ meeting on Saturday night. Church on Saturday? The matron would never let me out. But this time she did—there was always the chance it might do me good.

When I arrived in Colchester I had to pass the cinema, and there were groups of soldiers from the nearby barracks looking for dates to accompany them inside. Within a few minutes I got myself invited in and spent a pleasant evening, imagining Maureen waiting patiently for me at the meeting, and hoping that this would be the end of her mission to change me.

How wrong can you be? On Monday morning there she was as keen as ever, and in desperation I agreed to go to the next meeting. This time she invited me to tea first so I couldn't get out of it. I can't remember much—I know I was bored stiff—and when Maureen hustled me to the front at the end of the meeting I assumed we were leaving by a different exit. When anyone approached me I simply said, 'Oh, I'm with the group,' and they left me alone. I just managed to catch the last bus home, hoping that by now Maureen was satisfied.

On Monday morning Maureen told me that I was now a Christian and she would help me. Everywhere I turned there was Maureen. 'Have you prayed? Did you read

your Bible? Don't do that any more, it's not Christian.'
I tried, but I couldn't keep up with her. To me it wasn't
real. I enjoyed being naughty and I didn't want to stop.
I couldn't pretend for ever, and the real me just came
bouncing back. I stole a bike and got caned for gluing a
teacher to a chair, and finally Maureen got the message.
She was shocked, but then off she went to find another
victim.

Maureen may have had the best of motives, but her
singleminded campaign forced me to pretend that I was
something that I wasn't. That kind of pretence doesn't
belong in the church.

I was at an all-day prayer meeting once, where the
local churches had gathered to fast and pray for eight
hours. For medical reasons I have to eat regular meals,
so if I do fast it is only when God really lays it on my
heart to do so. By midday I needed to get something to
eat so I quietly left the hall and went outside. A group
of the young people saw me and offered to share their
picnic. They led me to a spot where they couldn't be seen
and unwrapped the food. Why the secrecy? Apparently
the local churches had been talking about fasting and
what a spiritual exercise it was, and the youngsters felt
they might be judged as being less spiritual if they did
not fast. I enjoyed my lunch with them. Their love for
God shone through their conversation, and their desire
to serve him put me to shame. How sad that something
that should be 'in secret' had moved from being
something you do without boasting to something you're
patently dishonest about.

If the church fails to become a place where we can be
real and accepted as we are, then we force people to act
a part. That's always dangerous. Where *do* they go when
they are really in need? Where *do* they turn when
things have gone badly wrong and they are in a
mess?

Everything's fine

I well remember the day I met Hilary and Vera. I don't
think I've ever seen a sadder looking couple anywhere.
They turned up for a meeting in North Wales, and how
Vera managed to get there I will never know. She was
recovering from a nervous breakdown and appeared to
be drugged up to the eyes. Hilary just sat wringing her
hands, and the suffering they had both endured was
obvious.

My mind was working overtime trying to understand
what dark secret these sisters could be hiding. It must be
something awful to have had such devastating results.

Both of them had become Christians late in life,
although they had always been avid churchgoers.

'It was like coming home,' was how Hilary described
it wistfully. 'But then everything seemed to go wrong.'
By now she was weeping.

Everything that could go wrong did. The shop which
they ran together started losing money; both husbands
were being difficult; and Vera had the first of three
severe breakdowns.

'Did you ask your church to help you?' I asked gently.

Hilary looked at me in astonishment. 'Good Christians
don't have problems, do they?'

Sunday after Sunday one or both of these sisters sat in
church pretending that everything was all right, yet all
the while their hearts were breaking. How tragic.

I have often heard Christians commenting on suffering, and I wonder if they are implying that the Christian
life should be one of ease, with no problems or pain at
all.

But we have not been promised a life of ease; Jesus
tells us to 'take up our cross' and follow him. The cross
speaks of pain, and certainly the New Testament talks a
lot about persecution. 'Indeed, all who desire to live a
godly life in Christ Jesus will be persecuted' (2 Timothy
3:12).

I needn't go into all the details of Hilary and Vera's story, but they left that meeting totally different from the way they had arrived.

I have heard from them since, and their letters are full of hope. Vera is better and, while some of the problems remain, they are both assured of God's love and comfort.

I have met others who have felt the need to pretend— I have myself. How many people sit through services and, while all around them are singing and praising God, their hearts are breaking.

We should count it a privilege to suffer for Christ's sake, but in the West we don't know what persecution means, and we often deny its existence.

Let's stop pretending, and instead reach out to comfort and support those who are going through hard times.

Just as I am

I first met Colin as I was leaving a church where I had been speaking. He had been listening attentively in the porch, but refused my invitation to come in. He was gorgeous—shocking pink and green hair, tatty leathers, and a large earring in one ear. I was thrilled to learn that he was a committed Christian, but not so thrilled to hear what he said next.

'I just wish the church would accept me as Jesus has,' he said. 'I've been a Christian for three months, and I dearly want to be baptised.' He sighed.

'What's the problem?' I asked, hoping I might get an invitation to the service.

'I've been told I must change my appearance first. If I truly loved Jesus I wouldn't have coloured hair.'

I thought there must be some misunderstanding so I went to talk with the elders of the church. It was true. They insisted that Colin smarten up, take his earring out and change his hair. As Colin explained: 'I can't change my hair now—I have to wait for it to grow out. They didn't mind when I made my commitment to Jesus—and my hair was this colour then.'

Here was a young man wanting to be obedient to his new Lord and Saviour, and he was prevented by the church. How sad.

I meet many young Christians who feel that they are not free to be themselves. I know young people like to have a good moan sometimes, and they think that no one understands them, but something is happening here which I can't ignore. Much of my work with ex-satanists involves placing them in a church that will care for them, and while I appreciate that they will sometimes rebel against the discipline, many of them come back to me saying that the church expects them to change too quickly.

I know of one church where a lively youth group used to meet. It was a mixed group, mostly non-Christian, and served a very run-down housing estate. I had met some of the youngsters—their language was rough, they were prone to violence, but at least they were there. Some had even begun turning up for a Sunday night service. They were a bit noisy and they didn't stay for long, but it was a start.

Imagine my surprise when I heard that the club had been closed down, and the youngsters banned from the church service. The reasons? It was felt that the non-Christians might corrupt the others. Those youngsters didn't know who God is, they didn't know how to behave in church, and they are not prepared to sit and sing choruses. But they never will learn if we send them away. If we are going to use our church facilities to reach outsiders we have to be prepared for all kinds of problems, and we need to understand that young people will not change overnight, either their appearance or their language.

Not all churches react like that. I have some dear friends in South Wales who, on finding that a young girl in their church was pregnant, were wonderful. They encouraged the other youngsters to take responsibility for visiting, babysitting after the birth and generally taking care of one who on her own would have been very lonely.

No smoking, please

One of the most common reasons that people give for not responding to the gospel is that they won't be able to 'keep it up'. We may spend hours trying to convince them that it is God who does the work in us, but when they do come into the church we confront them with a handbook of rules and regulations. How dare we set standards that we ourselves can't achieve? God knows the right time and the right way to change lives. Part of our witness is when people see our changing attitudes, notice our serving hearts, watch us as we overcome bad habits. One of the first things that others noticed about me was that my language changed. Not overnight, but slowly I stopped swearing. Then my friends knew that something had happened and they were prepared to listen to what I had to say.

At one church, just as I was finishing preaching, I saw a group of youngsters get up and leave. Now I may not be the world's greatest preacher, but I didn't think it was that bad! I had been told to stand at the door and shake hands with the congregation, but in fact I went out to find the young people. I couldn't see them, but my nose told me where they were—hiding round the corner smoking cigarettes. When they saw me they nearly died, even burning themselves as they tried to hide the evidence. When they realised I wasn't annoyed we had a good chat. Some of them were already Christians, and two more responded right there and then and joined the family of God.

Smoking is not healthy, but if you are addicted to

nicotine a two-hour service is a long time. How important it is to show complete acceptance, and allow
individuals to work things out with God. I'm not
condoning smoking. But is it a bigger sin than envy,
pride, jealousy? Young people are often very honest and
open about themselves and their sin. We need to
encourage and help them to grow and to change for the
better, but we need to recognise that this is the work of
the Holy Spirit. How it must hurt God when our hearts
are hardened against one another.

Putting on our Sunday best

The more I travel the more I see the need for reality in
the church. We are human beings and we can't deny our
humanity in order to appear more spiritual.

We all know that sinking feeling when someone is
coming to stay at our home for the weekend; that feeling
that we must have everything perfect for them. We
spring clean the house, tidy up the airing cupboard in
case someone should peep into it, dare the children to
misbehave and de-flea the dog. From the moment our
guests arrive we are anxious that everything should go
right. The tension builds up, the kids are naughty, the
dog misbehaves and then the Yorkshire pudding won't
rise. We just manage to keep a lid on things until our
guests leave, and then we flop down in tears, physically
and emotionally exhausted.

Is our church like that, too? Will people feel free to
be themselves? Can we relax with others and share with
them? Will they feel free to drop in and have a cup of tea
with us?

That is the sort of church we need to create, allowing
each one, peculiar habits and all, to be individuals,
but members of the same family where there is no
judgement but only love and acceptance. Like the
old hymn says:

Just as I am, without one plea
But that thy blood was shed for me,
And that thou bid'st me come to thee:
O Lamb of God, I come.

C. Elliot (1789–1871)

9

The Need to Fail

The first time I was invited to appear on a television programme I was thrilled to bits. By the end of the programme I was in tears.

I had been invited to a televised debate with witches; I only had the microphone for a couple of seconds, and said nothing of value at all. Afterwards a gentleman came and said very gently, 'God is going to give you another opportunity, but you must have the right motive.' I knew immediately what he meant. My heart had been puffed up with pride—all I wanted to do was discredit the witches. I had thought I was God's gift to the church, and I found out the hard way that God could not use me if all I wanted was self glory. I didn't even have love in my heart; I was full of scorn. I felt a complete failure.

My first temptation was to blame Satan for it; but how could I blame him for my own attitudes? I was the one who wanted to embarrass the witches; I was the one who thought I had all the answers.

God used that incident to teach me. He enabled me to repent, and helped me to see people as he sees them. I had to re-think what the television programme was for, and to realise that in everything I am to bring glory to God—not Audrey Harper.

A fortnight later another programme came up, and I have done many more since, but now I spend time in prayer before each one, asking God what he wants to achieve, and whether he can use me.

The fellowship of failures

All of us have failed at some point in our lives, but if we can submit the failure to God and allow ourselves to learn from it, we can be forgiven and God can use us again. And if we try to kid ourselves that we can live a completely failure-free life, we are no better than the pedlars of the occult who promise a life of unbroken success and power from here on.

Anyway, we are in good company. The Bible tells of many who failed miserably and yet were used mightily by God. The 'communion of saints' is just as much a 'fellowship of failures'. Our failures may have lasting consequences, but our relationship with God can always be restored.

King David was a man chosen by God. He took over as king, first of Judah and eventually over all Israel, and his story is told in 1 and 2 Samuel. Everything he turned his hand to was blessed, and the country benefited as David walked in obedience to God.

Then things began to go wrong. David caught sight of a woman and he wanted her: he gave in to lust. He had a choice—it was no good blaming anyone else. When the woman became pregnant David arranged to get her husband murdered. David may have felt he was fooling the people, but he couldn't fool God, and God set about exposing David's sin.

God used Nathan to show David what he had done. What a shock for David when he is faced with reality, and understands that it is he who deserves the death penalty. But he confessed his sin to Nathan, and although he lost the child that his wife had borne him, his life was spared.

Like many others before and after him, David's

problem was a sexual one. Christians are not immune to temptation, and over the last few years many well-known names have found themselves in the headlines. In the church we need to be aware that our own youngsters face the same sexual temptations, and to help them come to terms with themselves and to avoid difficult situations. I have helped several youngsters who, having indulged in sexual activity, feel complete failures and suffer terrible guilt. Are we giving them enough guidance?

I well remember one youth worker ringing me in despair. She had asked the church whether I could go and talk to the older youth group about the occult, and also to cover drug-related problems. The church had refused; just as they had when she wanted to discuss abortion, video nasties, and several other subjects that the youngsters themselves were asking about. I can appreciate people being wary, but to refuse to talk about *anything*? We must discuss openly the issues that are on young people's agenda. The New Age certainly does.

The church needs to recognise that as humans we will fail, our young people will fail, our church leaders will fail. How are we going to face the failures that happen and make them count for God?

David's reaction to his failure was to confess it. And please note that he confessed to Nathan, not the whole neighbourhood. If we have a problem we need to be able to go to our church leaders and share and accept their advice, knowing that, unless it is necessary, it won't go any further.

An understanding attitude

Ted had overcome a drink problem, and for many years he was a shining example of the power of God to change lives. Then sadly he succumbed to having just one drink, and without warning he was again doing the rounds of the local pubs and being arrested for being drunk and disorderly. As soon as he realised what was happening, Ted sought the advice of his church leadership and willingly agreed to go to a rehabilitation centre to dry out. Now Ted had only spoken to the leaders—he didn't feel up to a full confession in front of the whole church. After a few weeks Ted was able to go back to his fellowship, and on Sunday morning he looked forward to seeing his friends. When he arrived he was devastated by the reception he got. Knowing looks were passed, and no one spoke to him. His heart ached, and his sense of failure was overwhelming. Ted wasn't asking the church to excuse him, but rather to understand and to help him.

When we fail we need to know the love and encouragement of our fellowship, to accept their advice and discipline, and to know that their actions and reactions are motivated by love.

Someone else in the Bible who failed was Peter—the fisherman who left his nets to follow Jesus. He spent three years with Jesus, learning from him and witnessing his miracles. He loved him. Yet when Jesus was arrested Peter, who had said he was willing to die for him, now denied even knowing him. Surrounded by a scornful crowd Peter was afraid and failed Jesus miserably.

But Jesus knew what Peter's reaction would be. He even warned him, although big tough Peter protested. Don't you think God understands our fears and failures too? When Peter realised what he had done he went away and wept, and I guess we all know that feeling. But in our failure we can get very close to God, and when we do overcome our fears and our weakness, we know that it is by his strength and not ours. And that puts us where we should be—dependent on God.

F is for failure—and forgiveness

We can be very good at judging other people's failures. The trouble is we only judge what we can see, and most of the time we don't see the whole picture. A very dear couple whom we had known for many years surprised us by announcing that they were separating after twenty years of marriage. I couldn't take it in. Twenty years is a long time, and I had assumed they were happy years. But it seemed they had been living a lie—putting on an act whenever they were in company. For the sake of their children they had managed to hide what was going on, and all we saw was a loving and successful family. But now the children were grown up and most had left home, and the couple decided it was time to come out into the open and tell their church fellowship what was going on. What made it worse was that both parties announced that they were getting married again to friends who were also divorcing. Apparently they had been having affairs for years.

It came out eventually that both sets of parents had disapproved of their first choice of marriage partners, and they had married each other against their better judgement. When I thought of all the mistakes, all the misery, all the years of unhappiness I was so sad. I love them both, and I still visit them. But they got a rather different reaction from their church fellowship.

They were asked to resign immediately and forbidden to set foot in the church again. It was made clear that the children were not welcome either, and as the older girl had arranged to get married there it caused a lot of heartache to someone who had done nothing wrong. The effect on the youngest girl was the worst. She could no longer meet with her friends or join in the church activities. She is now grown up, but she has not forgotten the attitudes that hurt her so much, and she won't go near a church or allow her own two children to do so.

We are not to condone sin; but neither do we have a right to condemn. If we imply by our words or actions that failure is unforgivable in God's eyes, then we will drive people away from him and leave them vulnerable to the enemy. God has promised to forgive all who repent and turn to him.

Learning the lessons of failure

Failure is caused by any number of things—disobedience, sin, lack of prayer—and we can only repent when we realise what we have done wrong and where the mistakes were made. It is all too easy though to fool ourselves by twisting the Scriptures and convincing ourselves that our attitudes can be justified.

I have a friend who has one desire—to serve God as a missionary abroad. For medical reasons she is not a suitable candidate for the overseas mission field, and none of the main missionary societies were prepared to accept her. When Kelly asked me for my advice I urged her to see that there is a vast mission field in this country. Why didn't she settle down and look for ways to serve God here? But Kelly was adamant.

'Go ye into all the world and preach the gospel,' was all she would say.

I watched in frustration as she convinced herself by various 'signs' that she was on the right track. She chose a country by sticking a pin in a map, drew out all her money and set off. Within twenty-four hours she was taken very ill and spent all her savings on medical care. She had to borrow the fare home—and was told not to return.

Instead of accepting that she had been disobedient, and that that was the reason for the failure, she began going round the churches begging for funds and blaming Satan for all the disasters.

Kelly never did go abroad again. But she has learned

nothing from her failure. God could be using her here and now if only she could face her mistakes and repent and be restored.

Accepting failures doesn't mean accepting failure

Unfortunately sin is often pleasant. We wouldn't do it otherwise. The battle is a daily one as we seek to draw closer to God and to learn to hate sin as he does. St Paul knew about this battle: 'For what I do is not the good I want to do; no, the evil I do not want to do—this I keep on doing.' How much we can identify with that longing to do what is pleasing to God and yet so often failing. 'What a wretched man I am! Who will rescue me from this body of death? Thanks be to God—through Jesus Christ our Lord!'

We need to be encouraged. If we really want to put down sin and face and learn from our failures we can— with God's help. We need to hold on to the promise in Philippians 1:6: 'He who began a good work in you will carry it on to completion until the day of Christ Jesus.'

10

Warts and All

The only way to understand love is to experience it. I missed out on love in my childhood, and as an adult I found it hard to respond to kindness wherever it came from. I reacted with aggression, hit out and ran away— it was easier to make myself unlovable than to let people get too close.

But when John asked me to marry him I said yes very quickly. To me, marriage had little to do with love, but it did offer stability, self-respect and the opportunity to be normal—to be like everyone else.

However, marriage was not easy for me. Having to think of someone else was not part of my selfish nature. I found it frustrating that I couldn't even have a good row with John because he used to walk out of the room and leave me ranting to myself. I spent the first six months working out how I could divorce him, but he loved me and gradually his love had a calming influence on me.

I decided to surprise him with a delicious meal one day—despite the fact that cookery is not one of my gifts. After a tremendous effort the results were disastrous. The roast beef had shrivelled up, the potatoes were rock hard, the cabbage was almost raw, the Yorkshire pudding was runny on the inside, and I had to sieve the gravy to be able to pour it! But I had laid the table for a romantic dinner, candles and all, and I had to serve

it—there was nothing else. I gave John his dinner and
crept out to the kitchen to cry. For a while all was quiet,
then John came in with his empty plate, put his arm
round me and said, 'That was delicious. Is there any
more?'

To this day I don't know what happened to the food.
John insists that he ate it all, but I have visions of
someone beneath our flat window getting soaked with
lumpy gravy. But it doesn't matter. I learned a lesson
that day that I should have learned many years before. I
began to glimpse what love was, and John was my
teacher.

Called to love

If only we in the church could learn to love one another
as Jesus loves us. If only we could accept each other just
as we are. Jesus said in John 13:34, 'A new command-
ment I give you: Love one another. As I have loved you,
so you must love one another. By this all men will know
that you are my disciples, if you love one another.'

What a challenge! Some people are easier to love than
others, but we are called to love everyone. Sometimes I
find it easier to love those who are not Christians. I can
accept their failings and make allowances for them. But
within the church we seem to expect so much of each
other. In the family unit we may not agree all the time. I
certainly have the occasional argument with John, and
I don't always approve of my daughter's behaviour, but
that does not alter my love for them. Whatever happens
they are my family and our love and loyalty are our
security. Why can't it be like that in the church family?

Living a lie

Jenny had been brought up in a Christian home and had
made a commitment at an early age. She was happy and

well liked in the church where her parents held posts of responsibility. At eighteen Jenny left home to continue her studies, and found herself in a completely different world. It was alien to her, but she followed the crowd and kept up with them. She didn't find a Christian fellowship at first, and the longer she left it the more difficult it became. There was so much on offer, and soon Jenny was out every night with the girls and drinking rather more than she knew how to handle. To avoid always being drunk, she began to experiment with drugs. Of course, the people at home mustn't know, so whenever Jenny went home she became the good Jenny they knew, attending church and sharing with no one what was really going on. She was living two lives and beginning to wonder which one was the real Jenny.

By the time I met her she had almost dropped out of college, and she spent most of her time in a dingy flat in London. She had still not told her parents, and she pleaded with me to help her do it. I had to contact them—Jenny was facing a court case for possession of drugs. They were shocked, but relieved to know the worst. It was a painful time for them all, but they were able to talk things through, and at least Jenny didn't have to pretend any more.

Jenny's parents turned to their church for help, and then they learned what rejection meant. Instead of privately seeing the family and praying with them, the church leadership allowed the whole affair to be public knowledge. The gossips did the rest. The parents were asked to resign, and poor Jenny was shunned when she tried to go to a service.

Where was the love of God's people at a vital time? The rejection was too much for Jenny and she sadly left home. Her parents now have no fellowship with the church and they struggle not to feel bitter.

Afraid of the church

When my first book, *Dance with the Devil*, was due for publication I realised how scared I was. I knew that God wanted that book written, but I agonised for days before it actually came out. I wasn't afraid of the satanists and what they would say or do; the death threats were frightening but we coped. I was afraid of the church. Would people read what I had done and judge me? And although many did write to thank and encourage me, there were indeed those who, in condemning the book, condemned me.

One of the weapons satanists use against those who want to leave the covens, is the threat that if the church knows what they have done and what they have been it will reject them. I know of two girls who took their own lives because they believed that.

A wolf in sheep's clothing

Jo nearly ended her own life. During her years in the coven part of her work for them was to infiltrate local churches and try to bring about their downfall. To her, Christians were the enemy, and the war was real.

Jo was good at her job, and yet as she explained to me years later, 'I didn't really have to do anything—they did it themselves.' All she did was to drop a little scandal into the church and watch as the congregation took sides. Prayer was forgotten, loyalty went out of the window, as people tore each other apart and made the church divided and ineffective.

I asked Jo if she ever found her job impossible, and she replied promptly, 'Yes, if their love was genuine I couldn't move. I had to get out.'

It was on one of her missions that God spoke to her. She couldn't argue—she melted. It took time for her to know complete freedom, but when she did, she was full

of remorse for the churches that she had helped
to destroy. Some were no longer in existence, but
Jo felt that she should visit where she could, explain
and ask forgiveness. The attitude that she encountered
stunned her, and almost sent her back to the coven,
where she would have paid with her life for her
desertion.

'Don't you ever come near here again. And you are
banned from all our churches in this country.'

Jo had to leave her home town, but she has now
settled, and her new church is glad to have her. She
knows a lot about enemy tactics, and spiritual warfare is
high on their agenda.

Of course we don't approve of what Jo did, and it is
right to be cautious, but why did those churches show so
much anger? Was it because of what she tried to do? Or
was it because she seemed to succeed? By all means let
us get angry, but let us direct our anger at the real
culprit—Satan. If our love is not big enough to forgive,
then we will push people into his grasp. We must use our
common sense and when such people come our way we
must accept them, but allow them time to prove their
new life in Christ, to grow and to learn submission before
we allow them to hold any position in the church. Jesus
calls his followers to forgive, not just once, not just seven
times, but seventy times seven.

Pressurising with prayer

I spend a lot of time picking up broken lives. Not all of
them have been involved with the occult, some are just
people who don't fit in. We all know them, don't we?
They've always got a problem, they never seem to
manage, they suffer a bit with their nerves. But Jesus
died for them too—dare we love them any less? I was a
problem not so long ago (some may feel I still am!) but
thanks to a caring minister, who looked for the reasons

behind my behaviour, I have a freedom that at one time seemed impossible.

Carol suffers from an eating disorder, and she was nearly destroyed— not by the illness, but by well-meaning friends in the church. She asked for prayer for her problem, several demons were cast out and she was told she was healed. But the problem continued, and rather than face the church and confess that she was still failing, she pretended all was well. But she was found out. Imagine her anguish when she was asked to leave the church. Because she lived in church property she was also made homeless. Is it any wonder that she became suicidal, feeling that God had turned his back on her?

A friend and I found Carol a new home and talked and, more importantly, listened to her. We soon realised that Carol had been sexually abused as a child. Her problem was not demons, she needed love and understanding and help to learn to love herself. Her church couldn't cope with not seeing the answer to their prayers immediately. Carol still has occasional attacks, but God still loves her, and so do I.

'Mind your language—the vicar's coming to tea'

If we are honest we have to admit that we all have some weakness or other that we battle with. We don't like admitting it, and we all worry about what others think of us. But we do need to learn to accept and be accepted as we are. We must learn not to get into the habit of wearing masks to each other in the church.

I remember once that John and I were in the middle of a blazing row. The doorbell rang, and still seething I went to answer it. There stood our minister, smiling and asking to come in. So on went my religious mask.

'Do come in. How nice to see you. Would you like a cup of tea?' Turning to John I said, 'Darling, would you mind putting the kettle on?'

How ludicrous! Two minutes before I was yelling at John, and now I was calling him 'darling'!

It reminded me of my childhood. If the vicar called at the children's home it was cucumber sandwiches, wash your hands and mind your language. It is so easy to slip on a mask, but we shouldn't have to. Within the church we should feel secure enough to admit that we don't all live completely victorious lives.

One of the problems is that many Christians cannot accept their own forgiveness in Christ, and it is therefore difficult for them to accept that others too are forgiven. So we judge each other, and we put barriers up between ourselves and those we think of as bad sinners.

When people hear what I have been and done they are sometimes amazed that I can be so happy. Am I hard and uncaring? Don't I ever think of those youngsters that I recruited into satanism? Of course I do. But I refuse to live in guilt. Everything is in God's hands and he has forgiven me and made me a new creation. I believe the word of God. Living in guilt only benefits Satan, and I have no intention of making his job any easier. I have been born into a new family and, though some of you may find it difficult to accept, I am your sister. God has welcomed me with open arms just as he has you.

One in spirit and purpose

I led a lady to Christ recently, and for a while she seemed to be growing. Then one day she came to me in tears. I was almost afraid to ask why.

'I can't stand the way the people in the church talk about each other,' she wept. 'They smile on Sunday, and rip each other to pieces during the week. It makes me wonder what they say about me.'

How could I answer her? I could only apologise for the church.

Gossip is part of Satan's plan to destroy the church. I

am determined that I will not help him. If I can't say something nice about someone, I'll say nothing. James warns us that 'the tongue is a fire, a world of evil . . .' (James 3:6). If we decide together not to allow ourselves to gossip to or about anyone, then we knock Satan's plan on the head.

And how much anger and malice have flowed through the church in the guise of denominationalism? The situation has improved in recent years, but Satan still uses our differences to drive divisions between us and put off those who might have become Christians.

I was taking a seminar once and was talking about the need for Christians to work together. We need a bigger army to fight in the war against Satan, and certainly in dealing with those who have been involved in the occult we need to be in close fellowship. Often these needy people will go round from church to church, looking for short cuts to freedom and sometimes setting one church against another. If the churches are already praying together they will be one jump ahead.

I was totally unprepared for the reaction I got.

'Are you suggesting we should have a united prayer meeting?'

'Absolutely!' I enthused.

'My church would be unable to join in,' came the response. 'You can't seriously expect us to meet with those who are not free in the Spirit.'

'Just because we don't dance, it doesn't make us any less Christian.'

'But you don't operate the spiritual gifts.'

This from a seminar of ministers. And I thought *I* had problems!

I have over the years visited many different churches, some charismatic, some not, but in each one there was fellowship, and in each one there were people who responded to the gospel. Surely that's what counts. God doesn't see our denominational differences: Satan does,

and he uses them. It is time we put aside the differences
and had fellowship together. We have to. People are
dying in darkness and without hope and we need to hear
their cries. We won't if we are arguing among ourselves.
We must become one army, bound together in love and
unity, fighting the one enemy.

> If you have any encouragement from being united with
> Christ, if any comfort from his love, if any fellowship with
> the Spirit, if any tenderness and compassion, then make my
> joy complete by being like-minded, having the same love,
> being one in spirit and purpose. Do nothing out of selfish
> ambition or vain conceit, but in humility consider others
> better than yourselves (Philippians 2:1–3).

11

Best Foot Forward

'I need your help. Please meet me.'

I wondered if the phone call was a trap, but the urgency in the woman's voice convinced me, and I agreed to meet her.

Rosemary surprised me a little. She was smart and articulate—certainly not the hysterical type—yet her eyes were filled with sadness.

'I want to write a book, and I need your help to do it,' she said.

'Why me?' Writing is *not* one of my gifts.

'Because you understand the subject. And I have to write it down or I'll never be free.'

'Free from what?' I asked, knowing that freedom would never come from writing a book.

Rosemary began to weep. It was painful for her to talk about her childhood, but she was living with it every day and it haunted her.

Rosemary was one of five sisters. Her parents were satanists, and they had drawn all the girls into the coven. At various times Rosemary had wanted to speak out against what was happening to them, but the other sisters had never agreed, and Rosemary's anger was directed at them as much as at her parents. From the age of two, when she had been laid on an altar and dedicated to Satan, to the age of thirteen, Rosemary had endured sexual and emotional assaults almost every week. Her innocence, purity and trust had been totally destroyed. Boarding school had ended the physical torture, but the emotional damage could not be put right.

Rosemary was now forty-five and married with two children. But she had found no peace. She had never told anyone about those early years, never unburdened her heart of all the guilt and shame, or had any help in putting her life together. She had tried to commit suicide twice.

I have often dealt with girls in their late teens or early twenties who have had horrific experiences when they were younger, but when I thought of all the long years that Rosemary had carried this terrible secret I wept with her.

'How would writing a book help?' I asked her gently.

'I want to get back at my parents,' was her reply. 'And if I can get it all out of my system, maybe then I'll find some peace.'

The bitterness and hatred that Rosemary felt were very real. How could I talk to her of a loving heavenly Father? How could I suggest forgiveness to someone who could only think of revenge? I knew that this situation would take more than a quick prayer to put right. Rosemary was living in her past and it was affecting every decision she made and everything she did. My heart went out to her. But for the grace of God, I too would be living like that.

Putting down the past

I well remember the battle I had to leave my past behind. I felt that I was too wicked for anyone to love—especially God, who I imagined as a judge on his throne, waiting to bang me on the head. Perhaps because I had never known the love of parents I found it almost impossible to think of God as a heavenly Father. When I tried to speak to him I would shrink in shame and run away to hide and to cry. Why should God bother with a tramp like me? But he does bother. 'There will be more rejoicing in heaven over one sinner who repents than over ninety-nine righteous persons who do not need to repent' (Luke 15:7). Just think, there is a party going on in heaven for you and me!

But good as it is to quote Scripture, it can't wipe out the painful memories. And God has not promised to wipe them out, though he has promised that one day he will wipe our eyes (Revelation 7:17). I quote Scripture because it is the one thing that Satan can't argue with. With God's help it *is* possible to be forgiven and to live in God's love.

One of the problems I had was that I was not willing to put my past down. I felt naked and vulnerable without it, and I think many of us are the same. My past became, as it were, my insurance against failure. 'Oh well, you realise of course that it's not my fault. With my background what else can you expect?' It brought me lots of sympathy and allowed me to go on as I was.

The first time anyone challenged me about this attitude I hit the roof. But the words burned deep into my heart and I knew they were right. I got right away on my own and I argued it out with God for a long time. I had known my old life for so long, and now I was being asked to put it down and trust God totally. I was scared.

The person who had preached about this had talked of Christians who walk about with dustbin bags on their shoulders. They put them down occasionally, but they always pick them up again. I didn't *want* to be a spiritual cripple, but unless I could put the rubbish down I could never walk in complete freedom. After all that God had done for me, did I have the right to refuse him? I suddenly found myself weeping. I really did love Jesus, and yet I was deliberately rejecting his sacrifice. And so I gave in to him and asked him to help me put the past down, to resist Satan and to look only forwards.

It wasn't easy. During the bad times I used to shout Scripture at Satan, and bawl choruses at the top of my voice at him. Having the prop of my past taken away made me feel weak and helpless. But he is faithful, and if we allow him he will make us 'a new creation' (2 Corinthians 5:17). The memories of the past may still be there, but they will not rule us.

Growing in grace

Ann was a pretty young lady who had an average home life, but without a great deal of love and affection. In her teens she became pregnant, and she gave the baby away for adoption. Just after that she was introduced to Jesus and fell in love with him. She made a commitment and gave her life over to God, but her Christian life was not easy and very often she didn't feel any different. She suffered bouts of depression, she continued to feel guilty and to think that she had let Christianity down. On the advice of her minister she sought help from a Christian counsellor.

The counsellor suggested to Ann that because of the lack of love she had experienced as a child at home the answer might be to go back in her memory to the moment of birth and to go through that birth experience again, this time trying to imagine Jesus there with her.

When I heard about this I must confess I was a little uneasy, but I am not a trained counsellor, and if this was all going to help Ann, then fine. But I do believe that when we become Christians God changes us and we begin—maybe slowly—to become what he wants us to be. Ann was continuing to go for counselling every few months. She told me she had gone through the rebirth experience twice more and really felt she needed to do it again. But Ann had been a Christian for nine years. Was she showing any signs of growing in grace and maturity?

Rather it sounded to me as though Ann was taking one step forward and two steps back. She was being encouraged to live in the past, to imagine Jesus in her past, to think about the past, to go in a trance-like state into her deepest memories. All this sounded to me too much like the teachings of the occult. Instead of finding strength and grace for the future, Ann was being ruled by the past.

One of the verses that was given to me just after my own deliverance has become very precious. 'Forget the former things; do not dwell on the past. See, I am doing a new thing! Now it springs up; do you not perceive it?' (Isaiah 43:18–19).

One of the difficulties I encountered in the church was that people would not let me be the new person that God wanted me to be. Some people have an unhealthy interest in occult matters, and I found that very often I was being asked to give my testimony on occasions where every person present was already a Christian. I was getting very tired, and because I was speaking about life in the coven so often, I was beginning to live it all over again in my sleep.

Satan will use anything to throw us off course, and I had to recognise that and to take time to find out what God's will was for me rather than doing what the church were asking of me. Let's beware of asking anyone with a powerful testimony to share it too often before they have had a chance to mature, to gain a grounding of good sound teaching, and to learn submission to the will of God.

Pressing on

God does sometimes want us to look back at the past. Often in the Old Testament he urged people to remember that he was the God of Abraham, Isaac and Jacob; to remember that he had delivered them from slavery in

Egypt; that he had done miracle after miracle for them. All memories that would encourage and strengthen them to go on.

It is not always memories of occult practices that hold us back; Satan is no respecter of persons, and he will take anything that makes us feel sad or guilty, anything that causes us to say to ourselves, 'If only I hadn't done that.' We cannot go back. We cannot change what has gone, but we can make sure that from now on every day counts for God.

> One thing I do: forgetting what is behind and straining towards what is ahead, I press on towards the goal to win the prize for which God has called me heavenwards in Christ Jesus (Philippians 3:13–14).

12

Fact or Fantasy?

Arriving home from a shopping trip, I noticed that my
answering machine was flashing. As I played back the
message I became deeply suspicious.

'Hello, Audrey, my name is Emma. I've been involved
in witchcraft and satanism, and I need a safe house to
live in.'

No ex-satanist would leave that sort of message for a
stranger to hear. I would have expected it to be much
more guarded, with no open admission of involvement
in satanism. I rang the number that had been left, and
was soon talking to Emma. When I suggested that I
contact a couple of churches in her area, she gave herself
away. She made it perfectly clear that I could only
contact one church because, as she put it, 'The other
churches don't understand me.'

I did ring one minister, and he confirmed that Emma
was known to all the churches. She was looking for
somewhere to live so that she could leave home, where
relationships were strained. Thus her request to me for
a 'safe' house.

With so much media interest and accounts of ritual
abuse filling the daily newspapers, it is important that we
learn to sort out truth from fantasy. It is not always easy.
Why do people like Emma insist that they have been
involved with such things? Why the lies?

Satan is the father of lies, and if he can get the church

running around after red herrings, he will. The Emmas of today are emotionally insecure and crying out for help. They have discovered that if they mention occult activities the church will give them all the attention they seek. They do need help, but not always the sort they ask for, and we can end up neglecting other aspects of church life with serious consequences.

I know of one minister who was getting demands for help at all hours of the day and night. A woman was using every trick in the book to get visits—including sending her daughter over to the manse with so-called threatening pictures. Eventually the minister became exhausted and his wife, by now very concerned, contacted me. At my suggestion they did some checking up on this woman's claims. It seemed there were already four different groups working with this family, including a drug dependency team and the social services. Satanism was just something else to add to her list.

Once the truth was known, life at the manse returned to normal and the minister could get on with the pastoral care of those in his church.

Lies and more lies

I was asked by the social services to meet and chat with a lady who had been on their books for years. Lately she had been making claims about ritual abuse, and as the social workers had no experience in this they were hesitant just to write off what she said.

I met up with Jill, and after half an hour both the social worker and I knew she was lying. Jill didn't know who I was, but she was actually quoting from my book Dance with the Devil. She contradicted herself several times, but she did finally admit that she had been sexually abused by her father.

By blaming Satan, Jill was able to talk about an

experience that had kept her in bondage for years—but it wasn't satanism.

Becky's attitude was very different. She was another one referred to me by the social services. Shy and retiring, she would hardly speak about herself at all. It took several sessions just to get to know her, and almost twelve months before she trusted me enough to share her experiences. Her physical condition was a proven fact, but the possibility of ritual abuse had never been discussed. I had heard similar stories before, but it was the small, often unimportant details— details that no one outside satanism could possibly know or have gleaned from books—that helped me to understand.

So how can we know where someone is coming from? I have been asked many times to explain the behaviour of those who are receiving ministry. Why are they so hostile? Why do they continue to mutilate themselves? Why the dramatics and the threats?

For years these dear people have been told, and really believe, that they are unlovable. That belief cannot change overnight. If anything they will want to try and destroy any love that is shown to them. They do not love themselves, they are afraid of rejection, and they prefer to feel in control of a relationship. That is why they sometimes hurt or cut themselves—if they look ugly, no one can possibly love them . . . .

The other reason is more difficult to understand. Within the coven the only way to appease Satan is to let blood. Every time these people feel threatened or scared they will resort to what they know. It is painful to see, but it is a habit that can be broken—just as any habit can—and as soon as they feel secure they will stop.

I still remember the time when, having been away from the coven for several years, I would suddenly feel very frightened. I couldn't tell anyone why, but in fact these times always coincided with satanic rituals. I was so desperate once that I cut up a newspaper and used the print to send myself a threatening letter. I took it to the police and, while they didn't catch the 'culprit', I felt much more secure with them around.

An old friend of mine had been looking after a girl who had been involved in ritual abuse. Claire had been doing well, but one day my friend called me in some agitation.

'Claire has just phoned me,' she explained. 'I rushed over to her room because she said a picture had just appeared on her wall. Audrey, it really is awful—and it's done in blood!'

'Have you actually checked that it is blood?' I asked her.

'Well, no, I haven't. Do you want me to?'

'Yes, please.'

I was confident I knew what she would find, but it was important for her to discover for herself.

'It's lipstick!' My friend sounded relieved. 'But why . . .?'

I arranged to meet them both so that we could discuss it. My heart went out to Claire, but I knew she had to face up to what she had done. Gently I asked her what had happened, and tearfully she explained.

'I was scared and uneasy and I didn't know why. I couldn't put it into words, so I drew the picture. It was the only way I could think of to make sure I wouldn't be on my own all the evening.'

Claire's fear was very real, and the date coincided with a ceremony that she had endured for seven years—of course it upset her. By getting together Claire and her helper learned a great deal. Their mutual understanding now meant that Claire could ask for help without having to invent a reason, and my friend had a list of dates that would enable her to be available at the bad times without needing to be asked.

Free to do right

After my own deliverance I found myself clinging to some of the friends I had known in the coven. I even used some of the powers I still had, and appalled and frightened myself. Maybe God hadn't done anything after all. Or, worse still, maybe something was left inside me. In panic I rang my minister, and what he said then has stayed with me ever since.

'God has set you free, and if you want to live in that freedom you must shut the back door to the old life yourself.'

I had to choose. I had to use my own free will. One of my main concerns today is to encourage people in need to exercise their own free will to put the past behind them. If we imagine every problem is satanic, that more and more ministry is needed, then we will end up wondering when—or if—it will ever end.

I have never regretted my decision, but at the time it seemed frightening. I was being asked to give up what I knew and totally trust Someone whom I couldn't see. Some people can't cope with that, and the fear of the future makes them hold on to the past, however ugly that past is.

They may react by running away and, painful as it may be, we must let them go. It will hurt, and we will feel we have failed, but we cannot impose our will on others. They may not have reached a point where they *want* to be free, and all they will do is wear us out and disrupt our lives. It takes time to learn new values and to develop new habits of thought.

What you can do

If you want to help those who are in need, or who are asking for advice and support, here are some guidelines. These are not hard and fast rules, but I hope they will

110 DELIVERANCE MEANS LOVE

offer a common-sense and practical guide to anyone who wants to make themselves available to those with this kind of problem.

1 Never make a decision on the first meeting

2 Never suggest things yourself

3 Take notes or record interviews. Don't rely on your memory—it can fail

4 Always give the benefit of the doubt—until no doubts are left

5 Go over old ground at each interview; the story may not agree, particularly if it is made up

6 Ask for detailed information on any cult, eg rituals, gods worshipped

7 Don't rely on feelings, even if you have heard some stories before

8 Love and acceptance are vital—don't abandon them

9 Ask about personal changes in sleep pattern, diet, weight

10 Where possible, check details with family or friends

11 Watch for signs of paranoia—voices in the head, wandering from the point, not actually listening to your replies

12 Never go it alone. Enlist help, especially from a doctor

As I said, this is only a guide, and if someone has been involved in witchcraft or ritual abuse, more questions will need to be asked. Some of what you hear may be shocking, but please don't show your reaction to the person concerned; it may cause fear and insecurity.

If you realise that someone needs more help than you can give, don't be afraid to call in assistance. Draw a group together so that you don't carry the responsibility alone. Don't be tempted to rush into deliverance; much counselling is needed first and this will give you time to find out what you are dealing with.

If you have never been involved with deliverance before, or if you are in any doubt, call in someone to whom God has given a ministry in this area.

If the media should get involved, remember that it is our job to help Satan's victims, not prove anything to the press. I know how painful publicity can be, especially if the facts are not accurate, but if things are left alone a story will soon be forgotten. It is when we try to defend ourselves that problems get out of hand. I have learned the hard way that I do not have to defend God. If he calls anyone to make a stand he will honour that. It's a very secure feeling.

Satan has been defeated and God does rebuild shattered lives. But if we spend too long looking at the darkness we will miss the light. Each one of us needs to take time with God. It is his life that we reflect, and his love and compassion that encourage us to work with those whose lives have been blighted by darkness.

13

Like a Mighty Army?

Our society is in a mess. Violence, rape and murder have become normal, and we don't get shocked any more. Unborn babies are killed. Scientists are offering single women the opportunity to have children without a physical relationship. Young children are placed for adoption with gay couples. Divorce is so common that couples are being encouraged to draw up contracts to share out their property, even before they get married. Official forms now use the term 'live-in partner' rather than husband or wife. The young person who remains a virgin until marriage is the exception to the new rule.

Young people worry about the state of our planet. They use drugs and alcohol to help them cope with the stress of modern life. Fear and greed are the motivators of our society, and the only help that seems to be on offer is a false gospel.

There is a spiritual force in our land that is destroying all that is good and encouraging all that is bad in human nature. It is an evil that has dulled our moral sense and caused us to lower our standards, almost without our noticing what is happening.

God destroyed Sodom and Gomorrah because he could no longer look on their immorality. How much more do we deserve judgement, who have lived so long in the light of Christ's truth? I believe that God holds back his judgement because of the prayers of his people,

but surely the time has come for some action. We are at
war, and if we do not take up arms and begin to fight
for our nation, then it will be lost.

> For our struggle is not against flesh and blood, but against
> the rulers, against the authorities, against the powers of this
> dark world and against the spiritual forces of evil in the
> heavenly realms (Ephesians 6:12).

Satan is a destroyer; he is a liar; he is the one who dulls
our senses. It is him we must fight. We must kick him
out of our churches and our land, rather than simply
spend time patching up his victims. We must treat the
cause of our problems, not just the symptoms.

No more conscientious objectors

How have we got into such a state? Where is the voice
of the church—in society, or in Parliament? Why do
people not look for answers to the problem in church,
preferring instead to try out other religions? Maybe
because we have been asleep, or too busy arguing
over unimportant matters. But that must change now.
There can be no more sitting on the fence, no more
conscientious objectors in this war. The world is dying
around us.

If we talk about warfare, then many of us tremble at
the knees. It could be dangerous, we could get hurt. 'I'm
comfortable as I am, and my pew is warm. Besides, what
can one person do?'

The thrilling thing is that the more who actively
enrol in this army, the bigger the army gets and the
more effective we become. There is a place for every
Christian, no matter how young or old, and though each
one may be insignificant alone, each is vital to the whole.

Our motivation must be compassion for the lost. The
same compassion that Jesus showed when he moved
among people on earth and wept for them. We need to

learn how to weep for those groping in darkness, lost and helpless. And our equipment for this warfare is that supplied by God himself. Ignorance and fear must be overcome as we learn to use the weapons God has given us.

Training up the troops

One of my favourite Bible stories is that of David and Goliath. It is found in 1 Samuel 17 and is one that most of us know well, and even children can tell the story—a Sunday school favourite. People always find hope in it: the little guy can beat the big one.

The Philistine and Israelite armies stood facing each other across the valley, and every day the Philistine champion Goliath stood in front of his enemies and taunted them. He challenged them to send out a man who would fight him in single combat and so decide the battle. And each day the Israelites looked at this nine-foot high monster—and shivered.

Now David was not officially involved in the battle; he was running errands for his father and taking food to his three brothers who were in the army. His oldest brother, Eliab, was not at all pleased to see him, and accused him of neglecting his shepherding duties in order to watch the battle. What good would a young boy be in these circumstances? Let him get out of the way and let his elders and betters get on with winning the war.

Let's beware how we treat younger people in the church. It is so easy to feel jealous if someone younger moves in to our pitch, but we need to learn how to train them up for battle, not put them down. I am amazed at some of the people God is using today. They often don't look the part, but God knows every heart and he knows what each one is capable of.

The next time Goliath went out and shouted his taunts across the valley, David heard him. I think David must have felt angry at that point. He loved God, and had been brought up to keep his laws. How could the Israelite army just stand there and do nothing in the face of these taunts? 'Who is this uncircumcised Philistine that he should defy the armies of the living God?'

And so David volunteered to fight Goliath.

> Your servant has killed both the lion and the bear; this uncircumcised Philistine will be like one of them, because he has defied the armies of the living God. The Lord who delivered me from the paw of the lion and the paw of the bear will deliver me from the hand of this Philistine (1 Samuel 17:36–37).

Satan is seeking to destroy human lives. He is taunting us every day. How long will we listen to those taunts before we move, take up arms and fight? He is a defeated enemy, he has already been judged and will be cast into hell, and yet when he puffs himself up to frighten us, we go into mass hysteria and do nothing useful. Jesus won the final battle and Satan *is* defeated, but he still wants to take as many with him as he can. Instead of being afraid let us show him up for who and what he is. Why bruise his head, if you can kick it in? (Genesis 3:15)

Fit the armour to the soldier

David was taken before King Saul and asked his permission to represent the Israelite army in single combat with Goliath. Saul, wanting to be helpful, dressed David up in a suit of armour, but David couldn't even walk round the tent, let alone fight in it. It didn't fit him—it was meant for someone else.

It's possible for us Christians to wear someone else's armour. We get lazy, and we fall into the way of being carried by other people's faith, living off second-hand experiences of God and wondering why we are not overcoming our problems. We need to put on our own armour of God, to get used to wearing it. Only then will we become more proficient in the battle.

David went back to what he was comfortable with. He had proved the use of his sling and stones—they had protected the sheep many times and would serve him well again. So he collected his five stones and walked out to meet Goliath.

Goliath couldn't believe his eyes. Was the enemy reduced to sending out boys to fight? He taunted David and called on his gods to curse him. David's response in 1 Samuel 17:45–47 is an amazing statement of faith and trust in God:

> You come against me with sword and spear and javelin, but I come against you in the name of the Lord Almighty, the God of the armies of Israel, whom you have defied. This day the Lord will hand you over to me, and I'll strike you down and cut off your head. Today I will give the carcasses of the Philistine army to the birds of the air and the beasts of the earth, and the whole world will know that there is a God in Israel. All those gathered here will know that it is not by sword or spear that the Lord saves; for the battle is the Lord's, and he will give all of you into our hands.

David had complete trust in God, and he didn't doubt for one minute that his God would do what he said he would. We too serve the living God. Is our confidence at the same level? Faced with a giant I think I would be looking for the escape route and trying to stop myself shaking with terror. But we *are* facing a giant, and our confidence is not in our own ability but in God, therefore our faith should be unshakable. He has never let us down, and he never will.

The battle belongs to the Lord. We are his instruments, and if we are willing to move out in complete confidence in God then we can be sure of the result.

Be ready for battle

I often hear Christians making claims that appal me. 'Oh, Satan can't touch me, I'm a Christian.' 'I just ignore him.' Goliath made the mistake of underestimating the enemy and look what happened to him.

Satan is on the move, and each one of us has a responsibility to our fellow soldiers to be clothed in our armour and to be proficient with our weapons. So what is this armour, and what are the weapons?

We find all the details in Ephesians 6, where Paul speaks of 'the whole armour of God'. Not individual parts, but a whole. We need all of it, and we need to put it all on—deliberately and daily. We need the belt of truth, the breastplate of righteousness, the shoes of the gospel of peace, the helmet of salvation and the sword of the Spirit which is the word of God. Add to that the most important thing of all—prayer—and our armour is complete.

Be 'brain-washed' by the truth

Armour is designed to protect vulnerable parts of the body. A helmet protects the head. So it is with the armour of God. We have been delivered from the penalty of sin, and as we walk in obedience to God we shall know a continual salvation from sin and its effect. Satan's first line of attack is often to our minds. He is the one who accuses, plants false teachings, causes doubts; and unless we protect our minds he will have a field day. In Romans 12:2 Paul urges us to 'renew our minds'. What does that mean? Does it mean we have to become different people, quoting Scripture all day long? I don't think so. I learned gradually, and with great difficulty, that it means training our minds, disciplining ourselves to think about the things of God rather than allowing Satan to wander through our thoughts.

And for the rest of it? Work your way through the list and you will see that God has provided everything we need. And he has provided weapons too. The sword of the Spirit is the word of God. Here is our most vital piece of equipment, and yet as I go round churches I am often appalled by the lack of knowledge of God's word. People are prepared to listen to tapes, to hear a good preacher, but how few are prepared to spend time with the word of God.

> Now [these] were of more noble character than the Thessalonians, for they received the message with great eagerness and examined the Scriptures every day to see if what Paul said was true (Acts 17:11).

We have the Scriptures, and if we check out what we read there we can guard against being taken in by false teaching; and by reading the *whole* of Scripture, we are less likely to be seduced by those who quote *parts* of it, out of context, to their own end.

When Jesus was tempted in the wilderness, he overcame Satan by the word of God. You and I can do that too: not just by learning verses parrot fashion, but by reading and re-reading, so that when we need them, verses come into our mind.

Pray without ceasing

The other weapon that Paul tells us we have is prayer.

> And pray in the Spirit on all occasions with all kinds of prayers and requests. With this in mind, be alert and always keep on praying for all the saints (Ephesians 6:18).

When I first began to travel round to different churches to share my testimony, I found a recurring problem. Each time the day arrived for me to catch a train or a bus, one of my family would be ill. Sometimes it would be a minor thing, occasionally it looked at if it could be more serious. I used to feel dreadful having to leave them. I would agonise all during the journey: 'Should I have left them? Should I have cancelled the speaking engagement and stayed at home?' I would wonder if I was hearing God right. Each time I would arrive at my destination and make straight for a telephone to ring home and see what was happening, and thankfully they were always fine by then.

I never went on these trips without my family's blessing, and I certainly don't think it was their way of asking for help. So what was happening? I believe that Satan was trying to stop me from sharing my experience of God's power, and the way that he used was to attack the family. When we realised this we stood in prayer together against him, and we asked others to pray too. The problem hasn't happened since. Once we uncover Satan's tactics he usually gives up and tries something else.

There are many different areas to our prayer life: private prayer, family prayers, praying in a small group or a large meeting. It's good to look at these different areas and to see where our own weaknesses and failings are.

A lady came to me for advice. She wanted to know how she could be an effective witness in her place of work. There was a lot of anti-Christian feeling, and she didn't know what to do. She had been praying for two years, but when I asked what results she had seen she shook her head.

'Well, how many Christians are there in your works?' I asked, thinking that if they got together they could encourage each other.

'I don't know,' she replied. 'I haven't actually spoken to anyone about it yet.'

She was asking God to do something, but she wasn't prepared to be the answer to those prayers herself. I can't judge her, I don't know what I would have done in that situation, but I do begin to wonder whether some of us opt out of the battle before it has even started.

I wonder if Daniel prayed before he was thrown into the lions' den? I wonder if Shadrach, Meshach and Abednego prayed before they were thrown into the furnace? They may have known fear, but I am sure they affirmed their faith in God to see them through whatever happened. Which is what we need to do. We need to be honest in our prayers, but we need to trust God for his grace.

Often our attitude to prayer can be measured by our response to the answers. I was at a meeting once when the minister asked me to lead in prayer. There was a young man present whose arm hung limply by his side. He hadn't used it since an accident, and had been told that he never would. I prayed very simply for him, and suddenly his arm shot up into the air and he was shouting for his parents. I stood with my mouth open and total disbelief written all over my face. The minister quietly suggested I shut my mouth and not look so surprised—it wasn't giving much confidence to the others.

Of course I hadn't healed that boy. Only God can do that. But I was surprised, and I realised that if all my prayers were said at the level of faith I had just shown, then I didn't deserve to see any answers.

There are those whom God has called to be intercessors, and to whom he has given the gift of faith. It is an awesome responsibility to pray, often with tears, for other people, and often without seeing or knowing about the results. But that does not excuse the rest of us from learning how to pray. Prayer must become a way of life, not a way of opting out of action.

So we need to recognise that we are all members of this mighty army, we need to put on the armour of God, to take up our weapons, and to ask God to use us. We must be willing to trust him, to take his light into the darkness, and to march across our land, united in the Spirit and in compassion for the world.

The night is nearly over; the day is almost here. So let us put aside the deeds of darkness and put on the armour of light (Romans 13:12).

14

Compassion: Storming the Gates of Hell

Dear Audrey,
I don't know if you remember me, but I want you to know that I have been accepted into Bible college. I want to serve God full time.
Love from Pam.
PS Do you remember when we first met?

How could I ever forget? Pam was such a scrap of humanity I wondered how she had ever managed to survive at all.

I first met her when she was living on the streets. She had just been discharged from a mental hospital and had nowhere else to go. Her whole life seemed to have been a disaster. Her mother said even her arrival in this world was a mistake. When I met her she was dirty and ragged, and sold her body to support a drug habit, but behind the bravado was a human being who wanted to be different.

As our friendship blossomed, she shared more of her story with me. Her father had abused her sexually and physically for years, and her mother had watched it happen. No wonder, then, that at the age of fifteen she had left home for good. With little education her job prospects were poor, and if she managed to get one she didn't keep it for long. Her life went downhill until the streets became her home and survival her only concern. As she said herself, 'I'm a complete misfit. I should never have been born.'

I tried to share my experience of a loving, caring God, but Pam just laughed. 'Don't talk to me about love. I don't know what the word means.' She said it with such conviction that I wept.

I continued to meet her, and persuaded her to seek help for her drug habit, while I tried to find her somewhere to live. Not easy.

Twice Pam was thrown out of Christian centres. Her behaviour was so bad that she disrupted everyone else. When I tried to challenge her she became quite angry.

'What do they know about the real world? They live on another planet. I can't be like them.'

And yet she so wanted to fit in. Her only hope was to find someone prepared to give her a home.

A couple did come forward, but I felt they should hear what she was like first. It would have been more devastating if things had not worked out. Yet after hearing what I had to say, and meeting Pam, they were more determined than ever to give her the love she had never had. It took a lot of courage.

At first her behaviour was disgusting, and she was very difficult. But slowly a change took place.

'They really do care,' she said one day. 'Despite what I've done, they still want me, and are talking about changing my name to theirs.'

Only God will know the hours of weeping, the great sacrifice that this couple made. But we all rejoiced when finally Pam submitted her life to God totally.

Now, after two years of a wonderfully changed life in Christ, Pam wants to learn how to reach others with his love. What a wonderful encouragement to us all—to see God at work in a life that had no meaning. And what a reward for that couple who showed God's love when preaching could not have reached her.

If we, as the body of Christ, can be real and forgiving; if we can be moved with the compassion of Christ; if we are prepared to step out boldly and be obedient to his call; then I believe that we could become a threat to the forces of darkness that are invading our land, and a haven to its victims. Truly against such a church 'the gates of hell shall not prevail'.

Dance With The Devil

by Audrey Harper

She was the devil's dancing partner, and he wasn't going to let her go without a stuggle.

For years Audrey carried a dark secret. Anyone could see she was a drug addict; some knew about the stealing and the degrading life she'd led. But she could tell no one, not even those closest to her, about the coven and the horrors she had witnessed there.

Now Audrey tells her story, providing evidence of the reported rise in ritual and sexual abuse among adults and children today. The cold fear that once held her in the depths of misery has gone. *Dance with the Devil* reveals why, and offers hope to those influenced by satanism—as well as help to those who fight against it.

'The occult is hurting so many—including children. Audrey's honest and powerful story helps us to hear the cries of the victims and to understand what is really going on.'
—**KEVIN LOGAN**,
author of *Paganism and the Occult*

Kingsway Publications